165482

780.01
Buk   Bukofzer, Manfred
             F.

             The place of mu-
             sicology in Amer-
             ican...

DATE DUE

THE PLACE
OF MUSICOLOGY IN
AMERICAN INSTITUTIONS
OF HIGHER LEARNING

SOME ASPECTS
OF MUSICOLOGY

Da Capo Press Music Reprint Series

MUSIC EDITOR
BEA FRIEDLAND
Ph.D., City University of New York

THE PLACE
OF MUSICOLOGY IN
AMERICAN INSTITUTIONS
OF HIGHER LEARNING

by

Manfred Bukofzer

SOME ASPECTS
OF MUSICOLOGY

Three Essays

by

Arthur Mendel

Curt Sachs

Carroll C. Pratt

DA CAPO PRESS · NEW YORK · 1977

Library of Congress Cataloging in Publication Data

Bukofzer, Manfred F., 1910-1955.
    The place of musicology in American institutions of
higher learning.

    (Da Capo Press music reprint series)
    Reprint of the editions published by Liberal Arts
Press, New York.
    1. Musicology. 2. Music in universities and colleges
—United States. 3. Musicology—Addresses, essays, lectures. I. Mendel, Arthur, 1905-   Some aspects of musicology. 1977. II. Sachs, Curt, 1881-1959. Some aspects
of musicology. 1977. IV. Title. V. Title: Some
aspects of musicology.
[ML39797.B8 1977]   780'.01   77-4226
ISBN 0-306-77407-0

165482

This Da Capo Press edition combines in one volume the first editions of
The Place of Musicology in American Institutions of Higher Learning and
Some Aspects of Musicology, both published in New York in 1957. They
are complete and unabridged and are reprinted by permission of The
Bobbs-Merrill Company, Inc.

Published by Da Capo Press, Inc.
A Subsidiary of Plenum Publishing Corporation
227 West 17th Street, New York, N. Y. 10011

THE PLACE OF MUSICOLOGY
In American Institutions of Higher Learning

By MANFRED BUKOFZER

THE LIBERAL ARTS PRESS
NEW YORK

CONTENTS

THE PLACE OF MUSICOLOGY

In American Institutions of Higher Learning

THE PLACE OF MUSICOLOGY IN AMERICAN INSTITUTIONS OF HIGHER LEARNING

1. The Progress of Musicology

In the course of the last three decades the study of musicology in the United States has evinced a development that, in certain respects, is spectacular. Virtually nonexistent in the early twenties, it has since that time grown to be a recognized field of study in some of our leading academic institutions; and it is still growing. The rapid pace of this development can be gauged from a comparison of the number of musicological dissertations written in different years. A survey of *Doctoral Dissertations in Musicology*, compiled by a joint committee of the Music Teachers National Association (MTNA) and the American Musicological Society (AMS),[1] indicates the sharp rise. There were three doctoral theses in 1926-1927 and forty-two in 1950-1951. Moreover, only a few of the earlier dissertations can be said to belong to musicology proper, although they may have an important bearing on it. It is noteworthy that most of the earlier theses were sponsored not by music departments, but by departments of psychology, history, or one of the languages.

Musicology thus entered the American university by the backdoor, by way of established nonmusic departments. This is but a natural consequence of the fact that the recognition of music itself as an academic discipline was and still is a slow and sometimes roundabout process. Musicology has merely repeated the pattern of music instruction in general. The latter, too, entered the American university by the back door, either as an extracurricular activity or by way of the band, the choir, or the glee club. Once music had a foot in the door, even the back door, it could press for further

1 Edited by Helen Hewitt, Denton, Texas, 1952.

recognition. The irregular and somewhat "illegitimate" entry music and musicology made into the academic field is ultimately the reason for the widely divergent status of music in our academic institutions today.

The recognition of musicology, in academic and related circles, was slow in coming. This may be seen in the results of what probably was the first survey of musicology in America: *State and Resources of Musicology in the United States,* published in 1932 by the American Council of Learned Societies for its Committee on Musicology (formed in 1929).[2] The best-known musical periodical of this country, *The Musical Quarterly,* opened its first issue, in 1915, with an article entitled "On Behalf of Musicology." A new stage was reached with the founding in 1934 of the American Musicological Society, whose activities now include publication of the *Journal of the American Musicological Society.* In 1951 the AMS became a constituent member of the ACLS and was thus recognized as a learned society in the field of the humanities. Some members of the AMS are now also holding office on the board of directors of the International Musicological Society. This international recognition would have been impossible without vigorous activity and the appearance of a number of important musicological publications in this country.

While there is certainly reason to review with satisfaction what has been achieved so far, the actual development has nevertheless not fully realized the potentialities. Lacking a general program or plan, musicology has grown by fits and starts. It has profited, sometimes vicariously, from a larger movement, the academic recognition of music in general; but it has at the same time inherited certain problems of college music which have in the long run tended to impede its progress.

[2] American Council of Learned Societies Bulletin No. 19, edited by Oliver Strunk, Washington, D. C., 1932.

2. *The Recognition of Music in the College*

The recognition of music as an academic subject in the undergraduate college is a rather recent and, we should add, a specifically American achievement. Since the first World War there has been a tremendous increase in musical activity, both in the public schools and in the colleges. The almost incredible expansion in public-school music is undoubtedly an outgrowth of the vital interest in music shown by the American public generally. This phenomenon is unique. Only in this country has the idea of a general musical education been combined with the comprehensive school system of an industrial and democratic society. The sociological reason for this unforeseen expansion is not any secret formula for musical organization but the fact that the schools, especially those of the urban areas, offer a degree of mass education not equalled in any other country. It should be noted that the idea of musical opportunity for everybody was not prompted by technological progress, as has often been assumed. The phonograph and more especially the radio were developed as true means of mass distribution of music only after the idea of mass education in music had already been conceived and put into action. But their usefulness was seen at once and they have given the movement its tremendous impetus, undreamed of by its initiators.

Once the idea of equal musical opportunity was firmly implanted in the schools it naturally was extended to the colleges and from there finally to the graduate schools. The far-reaching implications of all this have not been clearly realized. Obviously, this type of musical education was not intended for the training of professional musicians, although this may not have been entirely clear to its early proponents. Its logical aim could only be to foster more intelligent listening habits in the same way as a general education seeks to produce a more intelligent human being. It is therefore the idea of music as a liberal art, of music as part of the humanities, that underlies the idea of mass education in music.

3.   *Education* for *Music and Education* in *Music*

In musical education two aims must be distinguished: education *for* music and education *in* music. The goal of the former is to bring the young and the adult into contact with music, to lead them to an understanding of and intelligent response to it, to enable them to have a broad artistic experience, and to sharpen the senses and the mind for cultural values in general. The musical experience just described corresponds to the experience of great masterpieces of literature and the fine arts. There is no more thought of making the listener a composer than there would be of making the student of literature a poet. An intense musical experience calls for a certain amount of education *in* music, all theories of certain music educators to the contrary notwithstanding. It is a fallacy to assume that musical illiteracy can be overcome purely by "talent," "intuition," and receiving inspirational lectures. The listener needs familiarity with the rudiments of musical structure, though opinions may differ as to the necessary extent of this familiarity. Education *for* music thus always to some degree overlaps education *in* music, but this overlap should not obscure the difference in goals.

Education *in* music naturally covers also all the technical knowledge an intelligent listener needs for a well-rounded education *for* music, but its aim is more limited and is that of a much smaller number of people. In its purest and highest forms education in music means the training of the three most specialized representatives in the field: the composer, the virtuoso performer, and the musicologist. Both the "cultural" and the "professional" aims are necessary and justified; though they differ in nature, they are in fact interdependent.

Education for music is an old idea. It is ultimately derived from the Renaissance ideal of the well-educated gentleman whose education would be considered incomplete without some ability in music. The importance of music in the general education of that time is perhaps best known to the humanist from Castiglione's book, *The Courtier*. It should be recognized that the idea of a general education that should include music was originally an aristocratic ideal. Indeed, some of our latter-day "educators" have decried it for this very reason as "undemocratic." They have failed to understand that in the course of the nineteenth century the social basis of general education was broadened and destined to become the essential support of an enlightened, democratic society. The transformation of the aristocratic ideal into a democratic one has not been a steady process and has not been free from contradictory tendencies. Further expansion of the social basis has raised the problem of mass communication in an industrial society. Considerations of quality, which should always be decisive in matters concerning education, are in danger of being replaced by those purely of quantity. Opportunities for good music are then confused with opportunities for any kind of music, good, bad, or indifferent.

With the shift toward the quantitative, the musical experience loses exactly those qualities that make it valuable from the cultural point of view. In other words, music ceases to be a qualitative experience and becomes a means of inconsequential entertainment. Overemphasis upon the idea of entertainment in the arts has indeed vitiated the fundamentally favorable opportunities of the present situation. But even if education for music has not been turned to the best account, its underlying idea is sound and belongs to the best tradition of the humanities.

It is this humanistic background that determines the proper place of music in the college. Here education was from the beginning firmly grounded in the liberal arts, although music had to be satisfied at first with a marginal existence. For a long time music was regarded more as a genteel ornament than as a discipline, an attitude still to be found in a not inconsiderable part of the academic world. The recognition of music in the liberal arts college was inevitable, however, if the idea of a liberal arts education was to be taken up in earnest.

Sincere concern for the humanities was only one of the factors that brought music into the college. Coexistent with that concern was the development of vocational education, which manifested itself in the introduction of "practical" courses, such as home economics. The subsequent gradual rapprochement between the liberal arts college and the professional school has tended to blur the distinction between types of education that were at one time considered valuable in their own right precisely because they existed independently of one another. In music the result has been an increased and one-sided emphasis on practical music, identified essentially with performance or what has lately been called "applied music." This unfortunate term reveals a misconception of what music is.

The perplexing situation in which music instruction in academic institutions finds itself is due to the fact that complementary aspects have developed in opposite directions. The proper relations of these various aspects to the whole of music can be maintained only if the place of music in higher education is clearly understood. What with the prevailing confusion concerning the integration of music among the other academic disciplines, it is not surprising that a consistent policy cannot easily be formulated. Since the development of musicology in this country has been affected, a discussion of the place of the discipline and its function must first consider the framework of music instruction in which it operates.

4. The Traditional Curriculum of Music Instruction

The study of music as it is pursued in American colleges is customarily divided into four large areas: Theory, History, Performance ("Applied Music"), and Music Education. The latter two are newcomers, which in certain schools have begun to encroach on the traditional and more legitimate areas. The usual subdivisions are as follows:

A. Theory

    (1) musicianship, rudiments of notation, scales, ear training, and solfège;

    (2) written exercises and some keyboard practice in harmony (diatonic and chromatic); counterpoint (modal and tonal); instrumentation and orchestration; composition (sometimes regarded as a separate branch subject);

    (3) analysis (harmonic and formal);

B. History

    (1) survey of music history (as an orientation course);

    (2) history of single periods and styles (Renaissance, Baroque, Classical, etc.);

    (3) history of media and forms (choral music, symphony, etc.);

    (4) supplementary courses and courses preparatory to majors, usually called "appreciation";

C. Performance

    (1) group performance; vocal (choral, smaller ensembles); instrumental (orchestra, chamber music, band); mixed ensembles (*collegium musicum* and opera workshop);

    (2) individual instruction in voice and instruments;

D. Music Education

    (1) "methods" courses (vocal and instrumental);

    (2) courses in "materials and techniques" for elementary school, high school, etc.;

    (3) supervised practice teaching.

While not all institutions offer all these subjects with equal emphasis, the above outline includes nearly all that is usually taught in the undergraduate college. Graduate study is essentially a continuation of the courses just specified (with the exception of the most elementary ones) and offers substantially the same type of courses in an "advanced" form.

Where does musicology come in? Most frequently it is offered among the graduate courses as an added specialized pursuit. In some institutions musicology is introduced also at the undergraduate level, usually in the area of history and under the title of "elementary musicology." To assign to musicology a tagged-on position of this kind shows, as will be seen below, a misunderstanding of its nature, due to the customary division of the field into four compartments. This division has frequently been under fire, though not always for sound reasons. A large field must obviously be subdivided, and originally the divisions were no more than a pedagogical device to keep related material together and to teach it in a rational and efficient manner. What must be criticized is not so much the division itself as the gradual compartmentalization of subjects. With a decreasing circulation of ideas a hardening of the arteries has set in which has fatally affected the entire system. It is precisely the relation of one subject matter to the others that helps to give all of them their validity.

To relieve the situation, various remedies have been tried, without success. The same elements can be arranged in a different order, in a different time sequence, or can be combined in one big "integrated" course; but these mechanical attempts at improvement do not strike at the root of the evil. The divisions have their pedagogical justification, and neither their abolition nor their rearrangement can by itself guarantee results. It is the teacher of these courses who must constantly bring out the vital interrelations between the specialized subjects and thus lead the student to an understanding of them and, as far as possible, of the whole. A teacher unaware of them or too inarticulate to present them will fail to do this no matter how perfectly the curriculum may be arranged on paper.

What is actually taught in the theory as opposed to the so-called "practice" of music is not by any means a basic musical theory in the sense of an underlying philosophy, but a set of rules derived from an artificially restricted number of models. In harmony the student rarely gets beyond the rules derived from the style of the eighteenth and early nineteenth centuries. Similarly, the instruction in counterpoint is limited to what is vaguely called "strict writing" (modal counterpoint, roughly the equivalent of sixteenth-century style) and "free writing" (tonal counterpoint, eighteenth-century style). Little or no attempt is made to interpret these rules as generalizations of living musical styles, which represent mutually exclusive principles of musical structure. Yet these stylistic principles form in turn the basis for an intelligent teaching of both composition and analysis. The principles of stylistic analysis are valid also for the actual writing of music. Properly understood, analysis is composition in reverse.

The subject matter of music history embraces also the study of relationships, not of isolated dates, titles, and biographical anecdotes. Its first prerequisite is a thorough knowledge of the music itself. No amount of historical minutiae can substitute for it. For the understanding of a composition is at the same time both technical and historical, and the technical aspects of its structure cannot be completely grasped without considering the position of the music in its own time and in relation to earlier and later compositions. History without theory is as blind as theory without history is arid. In other words, history and theory, while easily separable in the abstract, are in fact completely interdependent.

Performance seems at first sight to be more self-sufficient than the two disciplines just discussed, but this is a delusion fostered by the huge amount of time spent on practice and external drill. The preoccupation with problems of muscular co-ordination and with memorizing a small number of pieces is the chief cause of the dangerous isolation of this art. The prevalent cult of the "personal" manner leads away from the music and encourages the performer to play all styles in the same manner. Only a few teachers of performance insist on the simple truth that performance, too, is subject to the laws of musical style and that interpretation must grow out of the music itself.

Another typical attitude is the unmusical separation of "technique" from "style" in performance. It can be illustrated most palpably by the student who told a well-known pianist: "I have acquired all the technique I need; now I am coming to you to learn style and interpretation."

Lastly, the unhealthy specialization in the subject known as music education is especially noteworthy. Surely the danger point has been reached when the knowledge of teaching methods becomes more important than the knowledge of music itself; when the alternative is posed whether a music teacher should be primarily a good teacher or a good musician; and when musicianship is relegated to "subject-matter orientation." It is true that there is ample room for improvement in the teaching of music, especially in the lower grades, but it is questionable whether this will be brought about by methods relying on faulty information. A glance at the textbooks which supply the "method" with "subject-matter background" discloses a frightening degree of studied or involuntary ignorance in matters of music history and theory.

Equally unhealthy is the tendency to stress the entertainment aspect of music and to pretend that music, or any other humanistic discipline, can be learned without sustained effort. Music education falls short of its objective if it fails to afford a genuine musical experience that will make the student like and understand music for its own sake. Instead, he is coaxed into liking music for irrelevant reasons which will ultimately work against music. What has just been stated about a good performance applies also to music education; it must grow out of the music itself. Those who believe otherwise treat music as though it were a bitter pill that needed sugar-coating.

The four areas outlined above are completely covered in almost no one curriculum. Two patterns of selection have become norms, that of the conservatory or professional music school, and that of the academic department of music.

5. The Conservatory and the Music School

The professional musician used to receive his training at the conservatory, which has a long and respectable tradition outside the university. It is only recently that it has been urged that conservatory training be offered also at the university or the college. This trend has been gaining rapidly and has led to the establishment of professional schools at universities under the name of "School of Music." The rise of the School of Music at state universities has had a profound effect on music instruction. The private music teacher and the private school, which so far had had complete control over professional instruction, suddenly found themselves faced with a tax-supported competitor. At the same time the School of Music could offer reasonably secure jobs to private teachers. Yet some large and distinguished conservatories continued to exist outside the universities as independent institutions.

Given its essentially practical aim, a conservatory or School of Music cannot make it its business to supply a general education any more than can, say, a School of Mining or of Medicine. The special arts and techniques required in these fields call for high concentration and thorough training, which take up a great amount of time. This means that the conservatory must take the cultural values of music for granted. In other words, the student at a professional school should already possess a general education or should be in the process of acquiring one concurrently at institutions best suited to this purpose.

Technical drill and constant repetition are necessary in order to insure muscular co-ordination and gradually make performance part of the habitual and subconscious make-up of the student. The enormous number of hours spent in practice is alone sufficient proof that performance is not a humanistic discipline, but it is nevertheless a rigorous and demanding study that has an integrity of its own. Much the same is true of the seemingly endless written exercises that are supposed to lead to mastery and to culminate in original composition. In sum, a careful distinction of aims must be made; the student may perform and write music in order to achieve technical proficiency or as a means of gaining an understanding of its structure and its cultural values.

The conservatories are geared to the musical life as it exists in the present and must satisfy the demands of orchestral musicians, singers, arrangers, conductors, and composers on all levels of music. The curriculum emphasizes mainly the doing, that is performance, and to a lesser degree the writing of exercises. This fare may be complemented by a dose of music education. Notoriously the weakest area is that of history which, if it is taught at all, is presented without proper relation to the music performed, and by teachers who lack thorough training. The music taught in performance courses is limited largely to the so-called "current repertory" and, as a result, the student's musical knowledge is restricted to a set number of "pieces" which go under the loose designation of "classics." It has often been observed that the broader aspects of musical literature are consistently neglected. This is understandable in view of the professional approach, though not excusable.

The production of competent professionals takes a great deal of time. The training of a virtuoso extends nearly always from early childhood to his twenties and even early thirties. For composers even more time may be required for the maturing of their creative abilities. This point, which every serious musician will readily concede, is decisive in any discussion of the differences between the conservatory and the School of Music.

The conservatory is not bound by a strict time limit. Its

master classes are open only to those who are ready for them
regardless of how many years have been spent in preparation.
But the often-voiced criticism that the discrimination of
musical styles is neglected or sacrificed to performance remains true. The danger that the conservatory may turn out
superbly trained technicians without intellectual grasp of
the music they perform is always a very real one. It can be
overcome only by a sound general education in music.

A School of Music, on the other hand, operates within the
normal four years of a college curriculum. Now, it is generally agreed among musicians that professional competence
cannot possibly be developed within this period, not even
with a graduate year added. Yet the Schools of Music claim
to do just this and even pretend to supply in addition some
kind of general education, all within the same time. The
consequences of this mixed program will be discussed later.
At present it will suffice to state that even under ideal conditions a School of Music can only make a pretense of carry-
ing out its program; it envisages too many disparate activities
over too short a period. There is an inner contradiction in
its conception that makes it a permanent problem child of
the university. In the conservatory, on the other hand, no
such contradiction exists—at least, none need exist.

6. The Academic Music Department

A Music Department, called "academic" (in the favorable
sense of the word), is primarily concerned with music as a
liberal art. Such a department stands on a level with the
other departments of the humanities. Music instruction at a
liberal arts college is based on the premise that an educated
perception of the arts is an indispensable part of a general
education. Music is introduced therefore not with the aim
or the pretense of training future musicians but of giving the
students a broad aesthetic experience in music. The general
courses are intended essentially for those who will form the

future audience of our concert halls and opera houses. Instruction is directed at the future supporters of our musical life, on which in turn professional musicians depend.

An understanding of the importance of cultural values must be inculcated early in the education of the comparatively few who will eventually dedicate their lives to music. Hence, the musical offering in a liberal arts college emphasizes the relation of music to the other arts and its position in history and society. Special attention is paid to the changes of ideas that underlie the changes of musical styles and to the different attitudes toward music in different historical periods. In the largest context it will finally show the principles and limitations of Western music as compared with those of the music of non-Western civilizations.

Music as a liberal art must be seen as a manifestation of the human spirit, as a part of the history of ideas. Hence, the technical side of music is taught not for its own sake, but as the indispensable means for gaining an insight into the workings of the musical medium, even as grammar gives insight into language. The grammar of music is only a part of a more comprehensive picture; it is the starting point for more specialized and technical investigations for those who want to become specialists, whether composers, performers, or musicologists.

No matter what the specialization intended, it can flourish only if founded on a liberal arts education. This objective justifies offering of the so-called "appreciation courses." These courses have been much maligned in the past and, unfortunately, often with good reason. If they teach music as a means of indulging habits of sentimentality or as a scheme for the support of the recording industry, they are indeed worse than no music course at all. Yet, the principle of a course in intelligent listening is in full accord with the conception of liberal education. Appreciation courses are therefore not only defensible but necessary. It is the choice of principle that matters. Bad teaching can be corrected, a bad principle cannot. Some institutions have recognized this and have assigned their most mature staff members to such courses. This policy will in the long run pay high dividends.

Performance also has its rightful place in the liberal arts college. It serves as a means whereby the student obtains first-hand knowledge of the literature of music and has the experience of performing in a group, an experience quite different from that of listening either to performance by others or to a record. It will make the student aware of the difference between active listening and that kind of passive listening which takes the form of turning on the radio "to concentrate" on something else. Performance courses also supplement the repertory of professional concerts, which give but a small fraction of the entire musical literature, and may be made to supplement the much more extensive one available on records. Learning the literature and participating in group activity form the ultimate justification for having performance courses such as orchestra, chamber music, chorus, and *collegium musicum* at a liberal arts college. But this does not mean that there is a place there for individual instruction in voice and instruments.

The position of performance at the liberal arts college seems paradoxical only to those who do not understand the idea behind it. The performances cannot and should not claim professional finish, but on the other hand the standards should not be deliberately low. The danger of taking a certain snobbish delight in flouting professional standards has not always been avoided. Contrariwise, performance in the college has repeatedly been criticized as "amateurish" on the tacit and false assumption that it is supposed to compete with or substitute for professional concerts. Judging college music by the yardstick of professional performance has done it great harm. It seems that the "professional's fallacy" exists only in regard to music, since nobody would dream of maintaining that only established dramatists and actors can understand Shakespeare.

Both the Music Department and the conservatory fulfill important functions, which need in no way be antagonistic.

The two institutions complement each other, and the author of these lines, speaking as one who has been educated in both concurrently, can state that he has greatly profited from both. Difficulties are bound to arise only when the one invades the realm of the other and when their respective means and goals become confused.

7. The Fallacy of the Compromise Solution

Music instruction at our universities expanded so rapidly that the question of its legitimate place has received little or no attention. Certain institutions decided upon the establishment of a School of Music, others set up a Music Department. Moreover, many institutions adopted a compromise between liberal arts and professional orientation, with the result that it made little difference whether the curriculum was organized nominally as a School or a Department. At some universities a School of Music exists side by side with a Department, each complete within itself. This always involves wasteful overlap and duplication.

The gradual assimilation of curricula is a peculiarly American phenomenon, but a most questionable form of singularity. The mixing of aims makes it impossible to pursue a clear policy, and the result may be that neither a general musical education nor professional competence can be achieved. The idea of offering a little of everything, which obviously satisfies only the requirements of the lower levels of music education, is an attempt at organized mediocrity. It can be overcome only by the most talented and determined students working against the system. If there is any prevailing danger in our national music education today, it is what may be called the department-store conception of music instruction, in which the essentials of both curricula are reduced and offered at bargain prices.

The department-store conception has taken many different forms. In academic departments it has led to accepting more and more credit points in performance toward a nominally academic degree. It has opened the college to teachers in semiprofessional courses who do not understand the function of performance in the liberal arts college.

In the Music Schools the same assimilation is urged from the opposite end. It has already been shown that the really fundamental error in the conception of a Music School is not that its aim is professional (what else could it be?) but the fact that in both its curriculum and its administration it is senselessly and artificially patterned after a college. It is a plain truth that the graduates of a Music School who are termed Bachelors of Music are neither competent professionals on their instruments nor finished products of a liberal education. Technical proficiency can be indicated not by an academic or pseudo-academic degree but only by actual attainment (which can be certified by a diploma). A good violinist proves himself not by a series of letters after his name, but by his playing; a composer does so by his compositions.

The external imitation of the college has in effect supplanted honest certificates by specious degrees in an effort to profit from the prestige of genuinely academic institutions. The notorious "upgrading" that has taken place at Music Schools has most frequently taken the form of interlarding professional courses with so-called "cultural" courses in languages, literature, and other fields. These are frequently but the window-dressing of an essentially unchanged, though watered-down, professional curriculum. The substitute courses have generally proved to be poor because there are lacking a special faculty, proper library facilities, and, not infrequently, a congenial academic climate. On the other hand, they take away much needed time from the professional training, so that the door is opened to what can really be called amateurish standards. Unfortunately, even some conservatories have followed this trend and reorganized themselves after the pattern of the School of Music. Here again the new "collegiate department," which cannot compare with the genuine article, has been established at the expense of high professional standards.

The unthinking imitation of the college pattern shows itself perhaps most glaringly in the adoption of the academic ladder ranging from instructor to full professor. A delicate problem arises when an Assistant Professor of Trombone is to be promoted to Associate Professor of Trombone. Since he was engaged in the first place because of his mastery of his instrument, it is difficult to find valid grounds for promotion except for quantitative ones such as length of service.

The compromise solution is obviously not the answer. A far more efficient realization of either goal can be achieved if each maintains its own identity and integrity. This does not mean that each should be isolated from the other and exist in a vacuum. If the collegiate departments of conservatories were really first-rate colleges on a level with others, the above criticism would naturally not apply. Some serious efforts in this direction are being made, but there is apparently great difficulty in getting rid of the idea that one can cut corners in a liberal education. A course in English literature, for example, makes definite demands which it would be preposterous to "adjust" to the level of future engineers or musicians. A liberal education is one and indivisible for everybody regardless of the future specialization of the student.

A Music Department cannot pretend to do more than give undergraduates a solid general education in music. No professional musician can dispense with it, since it is the foundation for the technical competence which he acquires at a professional school. This school may exist outside and independently of a university or may be run as a nonacademic adjunct in the University Extension or some similar organization working in harmony with, but not within the confines of, the Music Department.

8. The Place of Musicology in Music Instruction

It follows from the foregoing discussion that institutions in which professional and academic goals are mixed or confused will also misrepresent or misunderstand the place and function of musicology. This is why musicology is so often thought of as just another isolated set of courses that can be tagged on to any type of existing curriculum. Actually, musicology presupposes a liberal arts curriculum in music, to which it is related as a comprehensive method is to its subject matter. The scholarly study of music—this is the briefest and least pretentious definition of musicology—embraces all aspects of music and is therefore not an isolated field but an encompassing *approach* through which one may make close contact with any musical manifestation. It is consistent with this definition that musicology is a specialized pursuit or field only in so far as this approach may become the subject of a special study.

With regard to the four areas of music instruction, the encompassing nature of musicology means that the discipline formulates and furnishes the underlying ideas and principles which tie the separate areas together into a whole. Thus it is clear why it would be a mistake to advocate that musicology be added in the undergraduate college as an area additional to the existing four. To do so would only add to the general confusion. To institute a course in undergraduate musicology would mean that the student would be attempting to take the second step before having taken the first. This is the reason why it was necessary to outline the existing music instruction in such detail. Prospective musicologists will need all that is offered in the general music instruction of the college, provided—and this proviso is of the utmost importance—that the instruction is given not in a narrow and prematurely professional but in a humanistic spirit. Here again it is the attitude, not the external organization, that is decisive. Undergraduate music courses, if properly taught, cannot help being preparatory and introductory courses to musicology. Neither can they help giving the student of performance and composition a firm foundation for and a better understanding of his special interest.

The thought that the humanistic and the musicological approaches coincide calls for illustration. Evidently, it is one thing to teach diatonic harmony according to the rules of a textbook, in order to achieve proficiency in writing music, and another to teach it as a means for gaining insight into the structure of classical music. A teacher unaware of the stylistic limits and the historical position of the classical style and unable to show the changing relations between it and the preceding and following styles will not succeed in extracting from the rules a live musical experience. Now there is nothing wrong with "rules" *so long as* they are taught as generalizations of stylistic principles. These latter are the main business of musicology, however comprehensive the sum of its functions may be. Any teacher of music should be familiar with the principles of style in order to make his specialty musically meaningful, be it theory, composition, performance or education. This does not postulate that all music teachers should be musicologists, but that they should be familiar enough with musicological method to arrive at stylistic principles for themselves.

What has been said of the teaching of diatonic harmony applies equally to the teaching of the other subdivisions of theory as well as to "practical" music. Many teachers of performance and theory have the uneasy suspicion that musicology exhausts itself in the minutiae of music history and has no relation whatever to their daily work. This is due in part to ignorance and in part to the type of music history to which these teachers were themselves exposed. They are in this respect the victims of their own system. Stylistic criticism and the history of styles have been severely neglected in the past because they were taught by persons unfamiliar with musicological method and incapable of demonstrating the vital connections between music and music history.

An enlightened conception of musical theory, one that has profited from the results of musicology, goes far beyond what the term is normally supposed to include. Musical theory according to such a conception can be defined broadly as the method of explaining the structure of music. It has already been shown that only a very small segment of the musical structures of the past is taught at present in our theory classes. There are many others that cannot be explained by the commonly accepted rules of modal or tonal counterpoint or diatonic and chromatic harmony. This is one reason why music from other centuries—and even some music of our own century—proves to be such a constant source of embarrassment to our music instruction. This embarrassment would not arise if each musical style were to be analyzed and explained in its own terms and according to its own aesthetic standards. To deduce such standards and principles from the music is indeed much more difficult and laborious than is the application of ready-made schemes. That it helps in this task is one of the immensely "practical" values of musicology.

9. Music and Musicology

The relation of music to musicology has often been discussed and sometimes in a rather abusive manner. Much has been made of the distinction between the knowledge *of* music and knowledge *about* music. The first is supposedly the domain of the musician, the second that of the musicologist. Like all oversimplifications, this is only a half-truth; if the division between these two types of knowledge were carried to extremes, the end would be absurdity, for neither can exist in pure form, divorced from the other. The identification of musicology as knowledge about music has been summarized in the joke "Musicology deals with all aspects of music except music itself" or still more briefly as "words without song." It has also been said that a musicologist is a *"musicien manqué."* Perhaps some musicologists are, but perhaps some composers are frustrated musicologists.

Actually, the large area of knowledge with which the musicologist and the musician deal is common to both; it is always knowledge of and about music. It should be remembered that "knowing music" is not the same as memorizing music. There are virtuosos who have committed every note of a complex work to memory and can start playing it at any given point, yet have no idea of its formal and harmonic structure. In the deeper sense of the words they do not know what they are doing, even though they may give "unconsciously" a creditable performance. The correct order of the notes is meaningless if one does not understand the relationships between them that turn a series of pitches into the potential source of an aesthetic experience. The study and explanation of such relationships are within the province of musicology.

The fallacy of separating the knowledge of and about music can be shown by many examples. We may consider first an unusual passage in the *Eroica:* the introduction, in the development, of a new idea in the key of the Neapolitan minor. The significance of this passage in Beethoven's total output can be grasped only if one "knows" a great many other development sections in Beethoven's compositions. This knowledge will enable us to draw conclusions about Beethoven's usual development technique. If we want to appraise Beethoven's contribution to the development of classical music in general we shall need in turn an equally broad knowledge of the developmental techniques of Haydn and Mozart; only the comparison of these three would finally enable us to make a valid generalization about developmental technique in classical music. Thus the observation of a single striking feature in a symphony may lead us step by step to principles and problems that are the essential subject matter of musicological research.

The masses of Palestrina offer another example. Recent research has discovered the fact that a considerable number of them are "parody masses": they are based on other compositions by Palestrina himself or by other composers. Now, if we study the music without knowing about parody masses and without examining the model composition, we may easily make the mistake of crediting Palestrina with music he borrowed from others. It is obviously impossible to evaluate a parody mass if one does not distinguish between original and borrowed material. Only on this basis can one discover how Palestrina improved upon his model. Indeed, these improvements reveal the true genius of the composer. In this case, who could make a sharp division between knowledge of music and knowledge about music?

Sometimes it is argued that all these considerations are irrelevant in the face of the one and only important question, whether or not the composition is beautiful or enjoyable. This position brushes aside all historical considerations and seemingly concentrates on the music itself. But the appearance is deceptive. This is not concentration on the music but on one's personal response to it. Any decision about beauty involves standards by which the composer should be judged, and these standards presuppose musical knowledge. If one misses the point of the parody mass one misses the point of its structure. If one lacks a principle by which to grasp structure, to raise the question of "beauty" is to become concerned with a matter for which one does not have the means for penetrating insight, however enthusiastically one may obtain a partial glimpse of the truth. There is always the danger that raising the question of "beauty" may give rise to a vague escape into the subjective and to a pretext for an anti-intellectual attitude.

The musics of different stylistic periods and of different cultures can only be judged by the standards they set themselves. A certain harmonic usage, a certain interval pattern, or the total absence of harmony constitute configurations of musical thought that can be understood only in their own terms. We must, in other words, grasp the principles by which any music is put together. The idea, recurrent through the ages, that musical understanding can be left purely to intuition comes to us especially as one of the persistent survivals of romantic thought. Upon investigation, this "intuition" always turns out to be merely the criteria and rationalizations unconsciously taken over from a past generation. The widespread resistance to modern music is a case in point, but an equally striking example is the romanticized conception of Bach or Beethoven, which has survived in certain quarters to the present day.

10. *Aims of Musicology*

The ultimate goal of musicology, like that of any other scholarly discipline, is understanding. Through understanding, music becomes a more intense aesthetic experience with wider and richer associations, greater sensual pleasure, and deepened spiritual satisfaction. Aiming at understanding, musicology has in consequence no axe to grind. It is not interested in "defending" artistic manifestations of the past or the present. It tries to discover all the forms that music has taken and sees each one as a manifestation of the human mind. The musicologist seeks and gathers all types of musical knowledge, regardless of whether they can be of immediate use. An immense amount of this knowledge can be turned directly to practical purposes, but the utilitarian point of view is neither the sole nor necessarily the driving aim of the musicologist.

It would betray a very limited conception of musicology if it were thought of only as the willing handmaid of musical practice supplying fodder for the concert hall and replenishing the repertory of the performing artist. The discovery and revival of old music is a genuine and very important function of musicology, but it is not the only one. Should we refuse to be interested in Handel's operas because they have not yet found a permanent place in the repertory?

The practical aspects of musicology change with the times, and what in one period may have seemed extremely far-fetched may in another become commonplace. When the complete works of Bach were published by the Bachgesell-schaft, its editors never dreamed that their edition was destined to revolutionize musical practice. The edition was intended primarily as a monument, and only secondarily for practical performance, yet without it Bach's works would not be as widely played as they are today. A good example is the amazing development of long-playing recordings—completely unforeseen by the experts—which has made available for the first time a large repertory of great music hitherto regarded as "obscure" and of limited interest. Indeed, the recording companies are now scanning musicological publications in search of things to record. All this goes to show that in musicology, as in theoretical physics, certain activities originally considered to be completely unrelated to direct application may suddenly be found extremely practical.

Like the scientist and the historian, the musicologist is bent on research, on the discovery and explanation of new material that will enlarge the fund of human knowledge and open up new vistas and new conceptions. He may point out that certain dynamics were not used in the Bach period, and in so doing he states a significant item of scholarly information. The question, however, of how the modern artist should apply these dynamics in his playing of Baroque music cannot be answered by scholarship alone. If the scholar tells the modern performer what to do, he becomes, in a sense, a practical musician himself and steps out of character. He is then not satisfied with the investigation of facts, but draws conclusions for musical practice that cannot be proved historically. Many a notable musicological work contains such judgments, but the good musicologist must be aware of the fine line of demarcation that separates the investigation from the interpretation of his material.

The charge has been made that to the historian any and all events are equally important and that similarly the music historian must impartially consider both good and bad music. Now, the mass of music assiduously collected by the music historians is only the raw material of music history. Works of uneven value exist in the history of art as well as in the history of music. The musicologist must be able to strike a balance between the historical and the artistic importance of a composition, and these by no means always coincide.

Through emphasis and selection, the musicologist consciously or unconsciously makes aesthetic judgments that reflect his own time and temperament. The evaluation of musical standards varies with each generation or each period. Informed attitudes towards the music of famous composers are not constants but variables. The masterworks of the past do not change, yet they mean something new to each generation. It has rightly been said that histories must be rewritten every thirty years, and it should be added that periodic revaluation is needed even more urgently in the case of musical styles.

There is a curious and noteworthy affinity between methods of composition in modern and medieval music. Although it may sound paradoxical it is nevertheless true that by a subtle process of give-and-take an insight into the technique of Machaut will facilitate an understanding of Hindemith's music and vice versa. It would be folly to take Machaut as a "modernist" as some enthusiasts have done. The similarities must be recognized, but they are found in a different context and have a different meaning. Least of all do they prove anything for or against the validity of modern style.

How strongly the ideas of a period may influence musicological evaluations may be seen in editions of Purcell's music. Purcell's characteristic dissonances sounded "wrong" to Victorian editors and were consequently expunged from his music as "mistakes." To us today not only do they sound right but they account for much of the charm of Purcell's music.

It is a widely held and persistent misconception that musicology is preoccupied with old music and is essentially a pursuit followed by antiquarians. To the antiquarian the music of the past is good or interesting not because of its inherent quality but because it is old. Naive reverence for old works merely because they are not new and sentimental admiration of age for its own sake are signs of a lack of historical perspective. Artistic manifestations are not interesting curiosities salvaged for the present. Good and bad music have existed at all times, and the musicologist is interested in defining the difference between the two in each period. If he seems preoccupied with old music, as indeed he often is, it is merely because there is, after all, so much more of it. In principle, however, there is no difference in musicological significance between research work in modern and that in medieval music.

11. The Study of Musical Styles

If we examine the vast literature about music, we find, to the displeasure of many of us, that by far the largest part consists of biographies. The strange emphasis on biographical writing reflects very clearly the historical age of which musicology itself is a child and, more especially, the hero worship characteristic of the nineteenth century. Even more disturbing is the fact that the life of a composer has frequently received more thorough treatment than his musical works which, after all, are what make him deserving of a biography in the first place. There are, of course, good and valid reasons why biographies of musicians should be written, even if their music may not be worth while. Such works can indeed be fascinating psychological, historical, or sociological documents, though they are written from a point of view that is not strictly musicological, but from one that combines musicology with other disciplines. Certain biographies—such as Thayer's *Beethoven* or Newman's *Wagner,* to name only a pair of famous examples—are in effect painstaking historical studies that make no actual contact with the essence of music. Invaluable as these books are for the establishment of dates and other facts *about* music, so far as the masterworks themselves are concerned the biographers might just as well have been tone-deaf.

The overemphasis on biography has led to a large body of anecdotal literature which, though it has found great favor with radio commentators, is neither musical nor musicological literature and can only be designated as "musical science fiction." In recent years a shift of emphasis has taken place. Musicologists have begun to concentrate more and more on the study of musical styles. Indeed, style criticism must be recognized as the core of modern musicology.

Style must not be confused with mannerism or with a cliché by which a composer may be recognized immediately. It embraces all those factors that in their distinct configuration produce the unity and coherence of the music. Concentration on musical style means concentration on the music itself, but at the same time the stylistic approach is more comprehensive because it tries to formulate the musical principles that have activated styles in musical history. These principles never lie on the surface, but must be extracted by analysis. The configurations called musical styles transcend any single composition. Inasmuch as they are the generalizations of principles, they are abstractions, but necessary abstractions which permit us to see the unity of any one composition in the same way as the abstraction "oak" helps us in the process of recognition when we are confronted by a particular specimen.

The history of music must be seen not as a large portrait gallery of individual composers, but as a history of musical styles, and the latter in turn must be seen as a history of ideas. The ideas that underlie musical styles can be shown only in a concrete stylistic analysis which makes clear how musical elements are fused to the larger units that are elements in the world of ideas and how they achieve their specific effects. The point of this analysis—and one most difficult to understand—is that the same stylistic criteria may have different functions in different styles in spite of external similarity. The fact that change of context will induce a change of function calls for a contextual interpretation of music—which is but another name for stylistic criticism.

Contextual interpretation provides the only way to an understanding of the different modes of composition. The comprehension of former styles sharpens the senses for the modern styles, with regard to which a convincing and comprehensive theory is still lacking. By the same token stylistic investigations of modern music will help us understand the music of unfamiliar, non-Western culture.

A study of the evolution of musical styles provides the main factor round which the history of music can be organized. Their rise and fall determine the large periods of music history and establish the chronology of stylistic periods, such as the medieval, Renaissance, Baroque. This chronology constitutes one of the aspects of music history. There are other aspects which give depth and width to the linear chronological development. They are the styles of various cultures and nations, the personal styles of composers, the styles of certain functions (dance music), media (choral music), and forms (the fugue), and even the styles of particular works. All of these show the stamp of their respective period style, but at the same time their specific elements can be extracted and treated separately. The description of the origin and development of styles, their interrelation, their transfer from one medium to another, is the central task of musicology. Only the stylistic method will permit a correlation of music history with the history of ideas and the general cultural history of mankind, if such correlation is to be more than a loose comparison or an abstract parallelism.

12. Musicology, a Graduate Study

It will be gathered from the foregoing remarks that musicology as a specialized study must be taken up in the graduate school. The preparatory study in the undergraduate school should have awakened an awareness of music as a humanistic discipline and should not be used for one-sided specialization. The prospective student of musicology will need all of the available help his general education offers in languages, history, and other cultural fields. Time and again has it been observed that students holding the degree of Bachelor of Music are not adequately prepared for the graduate study of musicology. They lack languages, general history, and also the broad orientation in music and music history that a liberal arts college properly equipped for the purpose would normally offer. Lacking essential preliminary training, the student enters advanced studies with deficiencies that must be made up at an inordinate cost of time and at the price of personal disappointment and frustration.

A general education in music can merely lay the foundation of work which at the graduate level must be intensified and deepened. Above all a much more thorough knowledge of musical literature of all periods is mandatory. Only if this requirement is fulfilled is it possible to proceed to the main point of graduate study: the application of scholarly methods to the music of any period. By means of lecture courses and seminar work the student is trained in the technique of a stylistic analysis whose goal is synthesis. By means of research problems that gradually increase in scope, the student is led step by step to the point where he can make observations himself, examine and critically evaluate what has been written about music, and arrive at conclusions of his own.

The first stage of this process ends with a master's thesis, which should demonstrate that the student has learned to apply musicological method. Even if the thesis does not contain new results, it should exhibit mastery; for it is an exercise in method and not restricted, as is frequently thought, to music history. The method may be applied to any aspect of theory, music education, or performance. Masters' theses on practices of performance, however, are comparatively rare, because they call for special skill in the application of musicological method.

It is a common mistake to assume that the graduate work just described concerns only and exclusively future musicologists. Anybody active in one of the four areas of music instruction should be able to recognize the musical principles that connect them. Properly understood, the M.A. thesis is the touchstone of this ability. This is not to say that every teacher of music should necessarily hold the M.A. degree, although this would be desirable, but it does mean that those who have not acquired a comparable background are not qualified to teach music as a liberal art or even in a professional capacity, however proficient they may be in a purely technical sense. Many professionals are intuitively and vaguely aware of larger musical principles but cannot "verbalize" about them. In other words, they cannot formulate and use them as conceptual aids in their instruction. Lack of articulateness is always the sign of a poor teacher.

Advanced study in musicology proper begins only after the first stage has been completed. It consists of the studies leading to the Ph.D. and is in every respect comparable to programs in the other humanistic disciplines. It requires a thorough knowledge of representative examples covering the whole of musical literature, a thorough knowledge of the various research methods employed, of a large body of scholarly writings on music regardless of language, and of bibliography. Above all, it requires the ability to carry on independent work. All this should be tested in a qualifying examination, which should encompass the knowledge just specified and, in addition, should attempt to measure creative capacities. After this second stage has been reached, the student is ready to concentrate on a field of his own, which will be the subject of his Ph.D. thesis.

It is the stated purpose of the thesis to make a "contribution to knowledge," though it must be admitted that many fall short of this goal. Too often there is the temptation to confuse a quantitative addition with a contribution to knowledge. A misguided Ph.D. candidate may set himself the task of finding out how many minor thirds appear in

Beethoven's symphonies. With a little industry the answer can easily be found. Since so far nobody has been foolish enough to count them, this would be an "addition to knowledge," but certainly not a significant contribution.

The selection of a proper thesis topic requires care and judgment. It must be remembered that the thesis is an apprentice piece, which automatically precludes large topics requiring the comprehensive knowledge of the seasoned scholar. This is why treatises on the philosophical or sociological background of musical periods, fascinating as they are, are not suitable subjects. A problem more limited in scope, restricted either to a well defined period or a technical criterion, will prove the ability of the candidate much more efficiently. It gives him the chance to develop a limited problem within a larger musical context. Without such correlation the findings will lack significance.

It is easy to ridicule the titles of certain theses. The topic itself is no more an indication of quality or the lack of it than the paper on which the thesis is written. Only the method and the manner of treatment will disclose the value of the work, however obscure its topic. It is a widespread misconception that musicological theses must deal with abstruse subjects and obscure composers. If this were true one would be forced to maintain the evident absurdity that Beethoven would have to be ruled out as a subject in favor of his forerunners or lesser contemporaries, such as Stamitz and Hummel. It has been possible for this myth to arise only because it is relatively easy to deal with the lesser men who provide the background and milieu of the great composers. There is a dearth of up-to-date special studies on the masterworks precisely because they call for deeper insight and more mature judgment than can normally be expected of young musicologists who are just about to earn their spurs.

Nothing is easier than to amass new musical facts in a vacuum, as it were, and to become an "authority" in an obscure field within a comparatively short time by writing the "definitive" treatise on, say, "The concerto for double bass in the nineteenth century." Many amateurs know more about small and obscure points than any living musicologist, but they know them as isolated minutiae, without consequence and method, and they cannot derive from them any significant generalization.

It has been frequently, and often scornfully, remarked that musicological method includes much ballast knowledge which bears no relation to its subject. This charge is true, but it is true of any scholarly endeavor in any field. The discovery of a new symphony by Haydn or of a manuscript with medieval music is in itself a piece of nonmusical detective work, dusty library investigation, or just sheer explorer's luck. It has a thrill of its own, but it is certainly not a musical thrill, however important the discovery may be for musical practice. Those who profess to be concerned only with music should stop to think that the endlessly repeated scales and finger exercises of a performer constitute an equally heavy burden of purely mechanical labor that is certainly not musical.

While every musicological dissertation is oriented toward music, it should not exhaust itself in purely technical considerations, but should bring to bear the aids of scholarly method from the other humanistic disciplines. Of these a thorough reading knowledge of languages and familiarity with general bibliography are only the most elementary. More important are the critical evaluation of one's own premises, the weighing of evidence, and the ability to distinguish between fact and interpretation. Musicology differs from most other humanistic disciplines in that its subject is nondiscursive and nonverbal, and presents the constant challenge of how to "translate" music into words. He who has never felt and struggled with this problem does not know what musicology is.

13. Analogy to the Study of Languages

There exists a remarkable analogy between the study of music and musicology, on the one hand, and the study of languages, on the other. It is well to insist on the term "analogy" because language and music exist as two entirely different media, although they may be happily joined together in artistic form, for example in opera, oratorio, and the art song. Music has been called an "international language" or "language of the heart," but these are metaphorical phrases that must not obscure the essential differences in media. Music is a language only in so far as it is a symbolic system that must be understood according to its own "grammar."

In music instruction the area of theory corresponds to the teaching of the grammar of a language, even to the point of applying identical terms. In both one is dealing with the raw material: the "vocabulary," the grammatical "rules," and the "composition of phrases and periods." Normally, composition in language can make no more claim to being an original piece of creative writing than composition in music. Both are advanced exercises and, if pursued long enough, will lead to real fluency and eventually even to "originality." Instruction in foreign languages usually stops at this point, though there may be classes in nominally creative writing in Departments of English. Courses in composition are much more common in music instruction, especially on the graduate level, and presuppose a certain degree of creative talent. The analogy between music and the languages ceases here because the musical medium permits genuine creativity at a much earlier age than language or other media (Mozart!).

From the point of view of their history, music and language are not taught "grammatically," but serve as means toward a larger goal, the understanding of the "literature." This would obviously be impossible without some knowledge of the grammar. Conversely, the works of art can be and are being used as material for learning the rules. However, the emphasis lies definitely on the study of the literature. There are survey courses of stylistic trends, studies of selected masterworks, courses on one great personality, on one stylistic period, and on one particular form. Carried to the graduate level, the study is continued with increasing scholarly rigor and culminates in the same degrees. It is on this level that broad fundamentals of the field itself are studied. Subjects such as the relation between grammar and special problems of linguistics, the history of language, the history of literature as a history of ideas, and the comparative study of literature, correspond in the realm of music to the special problems of musicology: the theory and history of musical theory, the laws of style formation, and "comparative" musicology or the study of non-Western music.

On this highest level the problems and methods developed over a long period in the various branches of philology are in principle very similar to those of musicology. For example, the problem of establishing a reliable "text" in a critical edition calls for a kind of scholarship and raises questions of procedure and comparative method that are virtually the same in spite of the different natures of the media. Editorial decisions will ultimately be determined by considerations of style and form. Neither philology nor musicology should exhaust itself in the study of the laws of grammar and syntax. Both disciplines are directed toward the same end: a better understanding of the literature, the works of art themselves, which give the medium its cultural value and significance.

In the area of performance no direct analogy exists. This again is due to the difference in media, since a language can be read while music must be performed in order to be accessible. It is true that one can acquire a "reading knowledge" of music, but the ability to read a score and really hear it inwardly is the highest phase of a trained musical imagination, whereas reading knowledge is the lowest phase of knowing a language. Performance can perhaps offer a parallel to the actual speaking of a foreign language, which is not usually emphasized in our language instruction since it would involve the same amount of "practice hours" as playing an instrument.

It will be seen from the foregoing observations that music stands as one among other humanistic disciplines and follows logically the same pattern of instruction if it is conceived as a liberal art. If conceived professionally, it can no more claim a place at an institution of higher learning than does a Berlitz school.

14. The Pressure for Degrees

It follows from the definition of musicology as the graduate study of a humanistic discipline that the proper degrees for it are the M.A. and the Ph.D. The M.A. should not be considered and, as a rule, cannot be a research degree. It embodies only the minimum familiarity with musicological method that any educated teacher in the musical field should possess in some form or other. The Ph.D., on the other hand, is a research degree and is intended for those who specialize in musicological studies.

In the recent past the pressure for higher degrees in music has become increasingly strong as a result of the mixing of curricula and the wide acceptance of the department-store conception in music instruction. In their desire for easy academic prestige the Music Schools have embarked on a vigorous course of "upgrading" and have devised higher "academic" degrees in their "departments" of theory, composition, music education, and sometimes even performance. Musical theory is, of course, a perfectly legitimate subject for an honest research degree, but the specially designed doctoral degrees in "departments of theory" have lowered the requirements and replaced what they lack in humanistic discipline by professional industry. The degrees in other "departments" are even further removed from academic standards.

The question whether an advanced degree should be given

in composition has been hotly discussed, but mostly on a mistaken premise. The issue is not whether the advanced degree in composition should be called Ph.D. or Doctor of Musical Arts. The real issue is whether the university pattern can be transposed to a professional school of music without cheapening the standards on each side. The advanced degrees of professional schools are not, and are rarely claimed to be, comparable with their academic counterparts. A sampling of twenty dissertations from professional schools will prove this point better than any argument.

Universities that have succumbed to the glamor of professional schools find themselves in an impossible situation. They want academic personnel, but they need music teachers for their professional courses. The seriousness of the situation can be illuminated in a flash by a letter this writer received from a college president asking for a teacher of violin, "preferably with a Ph.D."

We have thus a vicious circle: academic institutions insisting on a Ph.D. for professionals and professional institutions insisting on a pseudo-academic degree because "there is a demand for it." Actually, the demand is artificially created by perpetuating the confusion regarding the place of music. This confusion has become a matter of vested interests with those institutions that are willing to satisfy the "demand" with cheap merchandise.

This writer has had all too frequent occasion to observe the desperate plight of music teachers who are caught in the squeeze. Perfectly competent professionals are suddenly faced with a demand by their administration that they acquire the doctorate if they want to be promoted. If they are advanced in years, they have neither the background nor the inclination to do scholarly work, yet they are forced to seek an advanced degree in order to protect their livelihood. Usually they lack the time to make up the deficiencies before they can start scholarly work. It is pathetic to watch the few who have the talent and who are prepared to make the effort at great financial sacrifice. The choices in directing their programs are (1) to make them see that the demand is an unfair and vicious form of academic blackmail; (2) to send them to an institution which has lower standards; or (3) to lower one's own standards. The last choice has proved to be good business for some, but the better institutions have had the courage to resist the pressure groups at the risk of reducing the enrollment. Here again, the real issue is not whether standards should be lowered or maintained, but how to remove the cause of the academic blackmail.

The results of such pressures are bound to be felt sooner or later in the nation's musical life. They can be seen already in certain state requirements for music credentials designed not for the advancement of music, but for the benefit of those music educators who take pride in always operating at the lowest common denominator. An education that does not consider the quality of the music it teaches is education against music, not for music. The pressure for specious degrees works to the detriment of scholarship and against the integrity of professional standards. It certainly should make us ponder that the majority of the outstanding personalities in our musical life—and here we speak of composers, performers, and musicologists—have built their professional careers on a liberal arts education.

15. European and American Plans of Instruction

The training of musicologists at American universities does not exactly correspond to that offered at European institutions, except perhaps at institutions in England. In Europe musicology belongs to the "Faculty of Philosophy" and comprises virtually no courses in "practical" music. Since university study in Europe starts at what corresponds to our graduate level, there exists no formalized curriculum in music comparable to our undergraduate instruction. On the one hand, therefore, the preparatory training is more flexible; but, on the other hand, the grave danger exists that deficiencies in the basic musical education are discovered too late. When entering the university the European student of musicology is expected to have received his practical training at a conservatory or with a private music teacher concurrently with his general education, but largely as an extracurricular activity. He may also continue his practical studies while active at the university. In general, the European student concentrates on his special field later than the American student. This has the advantage that he is usually better prepared in the prerequisites such as languages, general history, and philosophy, but the disadvantage is that his knowledge of musical literature and his facility in theory may be inadequate. As a result musicology has sometimes lost touch with music and has become a pursuit centering upon itself. A number of musicological dissertations give evidence of this danger by their tendency toward irrelevant abstractions.

The American system, on the other hand, suffers sometimes from the dangers, inherent in premature specialization, that manifest themselves in overdetailed descriptions that never reach general conclusions. The reluctance to proceed from details to broader principles is caused also by the fact that undergraduate students and sometimes even graduate students are spoon-fed too long.

From the social standpoint the American system has undoubtedly the advantage over that of Europe, where only a small segment of the population can afford university study. Since scholarships are almost nonexistent there and since, obviously, the most talented are not necessarily found among the privileged few, the principle of selection is not only socially undesirable but also inefficient. It is nevertheless a fact that both systems have produced excellent as well as poor results. This goes to show that any advantage is bought at the price of some disadvantage. Whatever the system, the shortcomings of the student must be recognized and corrected in time by the teacher. Even if it were possible to work out a perfect system there would always remain decisive human factors: the student's initiative and the teacher's ability to stimulate.

16. Musical Scholarship and "Science"

The scholarly study of music requires the same methods as any other humanistic study, but the musical medium calls for certain specific adaptations. Its main tool is the historical method. Even if the subject studied be contemporary music, it must be treated in a historical context. Being a humanistic discipline, musicology is qualitative research and can never abandon qualitative judgments in favor of quantitative data. Yet under the influence of the natural sciences a school of thought has developed in the humanities which rejects considerations of quality as unscientific and subjective. It insists on the "scientific approach" and will accept only statements that can be verified "objectively" by measurement and other quantitative methods developed in the natural sciences. It goes without saying that marginal areas of musicology such as acoustics and tone reproduction rightly apply the methods of natural science, being part of it. But acoustics is the science of meaningless sound. Aside from language, only in music do we deal with a symbolic system of meaningful sounds. Some of our musical scientists are unable to make this distinction and, moreover, confuse the reproduction of music with music itself. Small wonder then that a handbook of musical engineering, published in 1952, contains the following statement: "From an engineering standpoint the past history of music possesses very little of interest or value."

Quantitative methods are necessary also in the investigation of oriental and other tone systems, and in the investigation of tone quality which can neither be described in words nor indicated by musical notation. In these fields measurements are significant, but no amount of quantitative analysis can tell us why a tonal system was developed in one culture and not in another; nor can any amount of acoustical research explain the important position of the minor triad in our tone system.

The "objective" and measurable facts of music need correlation and interpretation. Music is a product of art, a man-made object and not an object of nature. Both natural and artistic objects can be submitted to scientific and quantitative methods of investigation, but the method of dealing with the object or of presenting the findings must be clearly distinguished from the nature of the object itself. Efforts to substitute measurements of quantity for qualitative judgments confuse research method with the investigated object and in so doing falsify its essence. In certain musicological dissertations a misguided reverence for scientific methods has brought forth a flood of statistical surveys, interval counts, frequency charts of chord progressions, compiled with great industry and even ingenuity. Statistical methods can be of value in the description of technical criteria, which are one aspect of stylistic criticism. But if stylistic criticism is reduced to statistical observations without consideration of context and of the configuration of elements, one never arrives at musical style, which is a qualitative entity. If the charts were no more than a concise presentation of the raw material, they would be useful; but if no attempt is made at integration the result is a mass of unrelated facts presented in a form that speciously apes the precision of scientific method. This is not musical scholarship but pseudo-musicology.

17. Musicology and the Other Humanistic Disciplines

Musicology is a relative newcomer at institutions of higher learning, and in consequence the representatives of other disciplines have so far not fully utilized the results of musicological studies. Formerly the faculty members in music were regarded mainly as representatives of a pleasant extracurricular activity. Now that scholarship in music has been established as a respected discipline in its own right, the musicologist has been received in the community of scholars. His presence on the campus has brought distinctive advantages to the teaching of the humanities. The musicologist is obviously the person to advise students in all matters relating to music and music history, and to discuss with his colleagues common interdisciplinary problems. There are few aspects of musicology that do not, in one way or another, also have a bearing on nonmusical matters. The close analogy between the study of music and that of languages and literatures has already been shown. There are large areas in the history of literature that cannot possibly be discussed adequately without bringing in music. Consider the songs of the troubadours, trouvères, and *Minnesänger,* in fact the entire field of medieval song in any language. Whenever music and words appear together, and they do all over the world, they become the subject of musicological as well as literary study. In the past such studies have been carried out side by side with little or no cross-fertilization, but more and more it has come to be recognized that topics like the art song, the Italian madrigal, the French chanson, the opera, the oratorio, and sacred music in general cannot be treated intelligently from the musical or literary standpoint alone.

The historian is interested in the history of music as part of general history. But he should not lose sight of the documentary importance of compositions for political and historical occasions, for dignitaries of state and church, songs of protest and censure, and music for propaganda, which are directly linked with political history. Church history and more especially the history of liturgy are obviously incomplete without a consideration of music.

It has already been said that musical biographies may combine a great many disciplines ranging from psychology to economics. Music can, for example, be regarded not as an art, but as a business and an industry. Indeed, it offers an interesting history in labor relations; the results of such studies are important for social and cultural history, but care must be taken not to confuse the economic with the musicological approach.

The interrelations between historical styles in music and in the fine arts have been recognized and studied more in-

tensively in the past than any other interdisciplinary relations, but much still remains to be done. This is true also of
musical aesthetics and cognate questions that call for the
correlation of musical and philosophical ideas. That music
forms an integral part of the history of culture is a truism,
yet it will be found that some of the leading books on this
subject pass over music with a few inconsequential remarks,
if indeed they mention it at all. The crucial position of music
in the field of anthropology will be discussed in a special
section.

Each of the fields mentioned has become so specialized that
no nonmusical scholar can be expected also to master the
musical side of his field. The situation calls for a joint effort
and close co-operation between the musicologist and scholars
in other disciplines. As regards university organization this
means much closer interdepartmental relations than pres-
ently exist. Joint publications of recent date by specialists
have shown how fruitful such co-operation can be, but unfortunately they have so far been the exception rather than
the rule.

The position of acoustics, physiology, psychology (including the psychology of learning and pedagogy) is not quite
the same, because these are independent fields in the natural
or social sciences, rather than the humanities. According to
an old and by now outdated classification these fields are
said to belong to "systematic musicology"; actually, they are
fields auxiliary to musicology proper, although their findings
—for example, a new theory of hearing—may be of the utmost importance for musicology. The quantitative methods
and results of the auxiliary fields find their corrective in the
historical conclusions of musicology. For example, acoustics
may define dissonance in absolute and quantitative terms,
while musicology will demonstrate that the same interval
has been treated as a dissonance in one style and as a consonance in another, regardless of its acoustical definition.
The raw materials of music, its nature and the way it affects
man, are the main subjects of the auxiliary fields. Their in-

vestigations cannot be ignored by musicology, but the results, whatever they may be, are subsidiary to the artistic use
of the raw material.

18.   The Study of Non-Western Music

The traditional humanistic disciplines have shown in the
past a determined and almost self-conscious limitation to the
patterns of European thought from antiquity to the present
day. The high cultures of the Orient and the lower and
primitive cultures of the rest of the world have not been
fully integrated into the general conception of man. With
the recent shift of interest towards Asian problems the shortcomings and limitations of the traditional view have become
especially clear, for example, when it was discovered during
the second World War that there was an acute shortage of
persons with a mastery of the languages of the Pacific area.
The modern conception of the humanities is no longer confined to an interest in Western European civilizations but
promotes the study of all cultures, high or low, as the best
means for an understanding of human behavior.

Although a young discipline, musicology has shared the
traditional limitations of the humanities—but to a lesser
degree. From the beginning it has included the study of
Oriental and primitive music or, in brief, non-Western
music. This special branch is known by the somewhat clumsy
names, "comparative musicology" and "ethnomusicology."
No matter what its name, the study of non-Western music is
actually a combination of musicology and anthropology and
requires the closest co-operation between the two. The study
also includes the musical folklore of Western nations. This
somewhat illogical division is a survival of the traditional
preoccupation of musicology with art music and of a correspondingly narrow definition of folk music. There have been
signs recently that these categories are now in process of
being revised.

Relatively few scholars have so far seen the need of entering the difficult and seemingly remote field of anthropological musicology, although the second World War suddenly brought into focus its immense practical importance. The methods of anthropological musicology differ from those of other branches in that they deal essentially with living cultures. Their music defies notation and lacks the kind of historical documents to which we are accustomed. As a rule, we are unable to discover much about the history of this music and must consider ourselves fortunate if we can piece together as much as a comprehensive picture of its present practice. Our methods are therefore essentially descriptive. This means that a historical study of the styles of world music is at present an unattained goal.

Non-Western music presents a great number of difficult problems that differ radically from those normally encountered in musicology. The basic musical concepts in Oriental music have almost nothing in common with those of the West, and as a result Westerners cannot directly understand the music of the East and Orientals cannot directly understand that of the West. The anthropological branch of musicology is attempting to collect the various musics of the world and deduce from them new concepts on which to base a proper evaluation. A comparison of the Western and the non-Western concepts will ultimately give musicology a truly world-wide inclusiveness.

We are as yet very far from this ideal. The gathering of non-Western music has only just begun, and we have as yet but a sampling of the musics of the world. They can be recorded only by means of phonograph, tape, and sound film, because they cannot be written down in our limited notation. The situation is aggravated by the paradoxical fact that phonograph and radio are destroying the native musical cultures more rapidly than the same means can record them.

19. Tools and Aids

The study of musicology cannot be pursued successfully without a minimum supply of the proper tools and aids. The most important of these is a good library, which should contain a comprehensive collection of the literature of music (of all periods), including the scholarly editions, and an equally comprehensive collection of the literature about music. These form the basis for any serious work in musicology, since they enable the student of the subject to gain a knowledge of musical styles. He must acquire a good "reading knowledge" of music, and for this purpose a large collection of recordings may prove a highly desirable aid, although it is not absolutely essential. However, recordings are indispensable in the study of performance practice, the tone qualities of old instruments, folk music, and non-Western music.

The collections of books and scores just mentioned represent the core of any library holdings, but they are not original research material. Manuscript scores, autographs, early prints of music, and early books on music and music theory constitute main sources for original research, and to these should be added the scores of modern music and recordings of non-Western and folk music. Certain American libraries have accumulated a vast amount of these materials, but the holdings of the average university library are usually insufficient. In the past, the musicologist has always had to travel extensively in order to collect his research material. Modern methods of reproduction such as microfilm and microprint have gone far toward eliminating this necessity. The progress made possible by microfilm has been tremendous. In fact it can be said that musicology in America began in earnest with this technological advance. It should be recognized, on the other hand, that microfilm does not completely remove the need for research travel and for the collection of new material on the spot. Scholarship cannot be carried on by remote control.

In special cases the needed collections of instruments may be available in the local museums of art or the museum of anthropology. Similarly, paintings or other representations may be studied for what they tell us about the musical practice of their time. Work in non-Western music requires the proper machines for recording and measuring intervals or for the analysis of the overtone structure. It is here that the help of a laboratory in electronics and acoustics will prove most fruitful.

The main musicological aids, however, will be found in the library and will include modern bibliographies, periodicals, and indices, which the high specialization in every field has made indispensable.

It should be remembered that even the best organization of library aids and the most complete research collection do not guarantee worthwhile results in scholarship. The student must be taught how to work with these tools and how to use them imaginatively. At this point the question of personnel becomes paramount: only a musicologist with ideas will be able to make the student see new musicological problems and teach him how to solve them.

20. Prospects of Musicology

Whatever may be said about musicology, there is no longer any need for justification or apology. Its rightful place at institutions of higher learning is assured. Its value is recognized by its sister disciplines and indirectly also by those institutions that feel compelled to offer degrees in pseudo-musicology. Imitation is still the sincerest form of compliment.

The introduction of musicological studies into the university must be planned with care and circumspection. It requires a well-balanced set of undergraduate courses leading up to graduate study. The latter ought to be contemplated only if the proper library facilities and personnel are available. Our best universities have proceeded in accordance with these points and have set an example to lesser institutions. It may proudly be stated that the young generation of American musicologists so far produced will stand comparison with that of any other nation.

The vast areas of work that still lie ahead in musicology can only be indicated here in their barest outlines. It is easy to prophesy that projects calling for interdisciplinary co-operation will receive more and more attention. The time has come when the musicologist needs his colleagues in other disciplines just as much as they need him. This co-operation will give the single disciplines new and wider dimensions, the import of which can hardly be overestimated.

The work of musicology proper can be divided roughly into six categories:

I. The discovery, collection, editing, and recording of new and previously unknown music. This is an ever present and never finished task that accompanies any historical investigation.

II. The writing of general histories covering the entire history of music or of the history of single periods and countries. Such histories should follow strictly the methods of stylistic criticism.

III. The writing of specialized histories of form and generic types of composition, such as the concerto, the symphony, the string quartet, the mass, the motet; and studies of particular styles and procedures, such as polyphony, homophony, and the fugue.

IV. Studies of special aspects, discussed in a systematic manner but approached from the historical point of view, such as the history of performance, musical instruments, orchestration, and notation; the history of harmony, counterpoint, music theory, music education, as well as partial problems of these larger topics.

V. Biographies emphasizing the stylistic development of the composer. Also archival studies which use the tools of the historian pure and simple. These include the local history of cities and regions, which sometimes yield remarkable results. Early American music furnishes a good and by no means fully exploited field of investigation.

VI. Monographs and stylistic studies of single works or groups of works by individual composers or groups of composers. The works of masters like Bach, Mozart, and Beethoven have received such attention, but a great deal still remains to be done.

It goes without saying that such studies will gradually shape and determine the public and professional attitude toward music and lead to a clearer and more profound insight into music altogether. The purely emotional and sentimental approach of those who teach and preach music as an entertainment will then slowly give way to a more enlightened and serious conception, such as has long been adopted without question in literature and the fine arts.

Many reasons could be cited why music and musicology are not just cultural ornaments without practical use. It has taken a war to teach us that if we wish to understand man's mind and emotions, a knowledge of his material culture is not enough. Music reveals to us man's inner life; its scholarly study is therefore of immediate practical use. Yet the utilitarian justification of musicology must not be overstressed. Immediate uses change quickly with the times and their demands may be ephemeral. The goal of the humanities, the understanding of man, although approached in each age in a different way, is timeless. The future of this ideal is also the future of musicology.

21. Summary

Musicology, the scholarly study of music, has developed in the United States in consequence of the general recognition of music in the college. Music instruction in the college is part of the general education in the humanities. Its purpose is not professional.

The traditional division of music instruction into four areas is basically sound, provided that the instruction is offered in a humanistic spirit. Specialization, be it performance or musicology, must rest on the foundation of a broad humanistic education. The Music School, externally patterned after the four-year scheme of the college, mixes professional and humanistic aims. The lack of a clearly formulated policy leads to a lowering of both professional and academic standards.

The study of musicology must be taken up in the graduate school. Undergraduate courses in music, if properly taught, cannot help being introductory courses to musicology.

Knowledge *of* and *about* music cannot be separated. The goal of musicology is to understand and to intensify the aesthetic experience. Attitudes toward music are not historical constants, and the musicologist, too, is a child of his time.

The study of musical styles is the most important part of the broad subject-matter of musicology. Concentration on style means concentration on the music itself. The musical principles that have activated the styles in music history can be extracted only by historical analysis.

The advanced study of musicology is comparable with the study of any other humanistic discipline. The analogy to the study of languages (philology) is especially close. The musicologist has been received in the community of scholars in the humanities, and his presence on the campus helps to advance studies of interdisciplinary problems.

The knowledge of man's material culture is not enough if we want to understand his mind and emotions. The study of non-Western music gives musicology a world-wide scope. It is an indispensable part of the understanding of human behavior.

Some Aspects of Musicology

Three Essays by

ARTHUR MENDEL   CURT SACHS

CARROLL C. PRATT

FOREWORD

These three essays are among the several devised by the Committee on Music and Musicology of the American Council of Learned Societies to advance the cause of musicology in the United States and to attract increased support for it. Different aspects of the discipline are herewith presented.

That musicology has a practical side there can be no doubt. That it can and should enrich the musical and artistic experience of all persons seriously interested in music must be the firm conviction of all musicologists who fully comprehend the significance and potentiality of their field. In the series of brochures sponsored by the ACLS Committee on Music and Musicology one of the foremost objectives has been to make evident the connection between the study of sources and their realization in sound. Arthur Mendel (Princeton University), distinguished as scholar and conductor, discusses musicology's indispensable function in contributing to the art of music. With admirable clarity he describes the service musicology renders to the practicing musician, at the same time persuading the latter that he can ill afford to neglect what the scholar teaches.

As musicology has broadened our comprehension and view of Western music, so too is it enlarging our conceptions of music in places far away in space and time. Music is not an art which is one and indivisible; it has flourished with many individualities in other civilizations and ages. The study of these musics, peculiarly expressive of the peoples practicing them, reveals a fascinating array of sociological and religious as well as artistic data. Curt Sachs (New York University) is renowned among scholars in this area of research. His essay describes the "lore" it is based on, the problems it poses, and the knowledge it produces. Ethnomusicology, an unhappy term (the author admits), is rich in scholarly rewards, for it penetrates deep into the spirit of man and illumines surprising patterns of human behavior.

Musicology, even in its relative youthfulness, must draw upon many sister disciplines. Though primarily concerned with the evidences of musical art, auditory and visual, it cannot exist without the aid of other learning. Its ramifications, indeed, are exciting to contemplate and consider; they spur the imagination of the beholder and lead him to view musicology as a many-faceted whole. Carroll C. Pratt (Princeton University), eminent psychologist skilled in combining several disciplines, writes forcefully on subjects ancillary yet necessary to musicology per se. They may not be the central concern of the musicologist, but he cannot avoid them if he wishes to attain learning and wisdom.

The members of the ACLS Committee on Music and Musicology (until September 30, 1956, called the Committee on Musicology) are: Jacques Barzun (Columbia University); Edward Downes (*The New York Times*); Gustave Reese (New York University); Leo Schrade (Yale University), secretary; Edward N. Waters (Library of Congress), chairman. (At the time these papers were planned and prepared, Manfred Bukofzer was a member of the Committee, Carroll C. Pratt of Princeton University was its chairman, and the undersigned was its secretary.) To this group have come the invaluable aid, counsel and collaboration of Dr. D. H. Daugherty, Assistant to the Director of the ACLS. The Committee evinces pride and satisfaction in these essays, written to broaden our understanding of the art and science of musicology.

EDWARD N. WATERS

CONTENTS

The Services of Musicology
to the Practical Musician

By ARTHUR MENDEL

THE SERVICES OF MUSICOLOGY TO THE
PRACTICAL MUSICIAN

Understanding is its own reward. Which is as much as to say that the pursuit of understanding—research, musicology —must be primarily its own reward. That the results of musical research are often of use to the practical musician should never obscure this fact.

It is the function of this paper to describe and evaluate the services of musicology to the practical musician. But I have no thought of implying that the value of any individual piece of scholarship or of any individual scholar's work is to be measured in terms of practical results—any more than by paying my electric light bill or my doctor I am measuring the value of basic research in the natural sciences.

What services does musicology render to the practical musician?

The most obvious and tangible are the editions in which musical scholars make generally available the music of cultures distant in place or (more often) in time.

This function has two parts. The obvious and basic task is to issue in many copies what has hitherto been available only in few or not available at all: old music in manuscripts, perhaps, or in prints originally issued in small editions and surviving only in rare copies; exotic music usually existing only in performance, not in notation. Facsimile, microprint, microfilm, and phonographic reproduction take care of this task, the scholar's rôle being mainly that of finding and choosing the material to be reproduced.

But the greater the distance—ethnological or chronological—that separates us from a given music, the more we need the services of an expert to transcribe it for us, from performance if it does not exist in written form, or from an obsolete or foreign notation that must be decoded for the musician of today. Phonographic archives of folk music, native and exotic, such as the one formerly in the Berlin State Library and the one in the Library of Congress, make available to urban Western Europeans and Americans the musical cultures of remote rural or exotic peoples, with which one could not otherwise become acquainted without far travels. A similar function is performed for the monuments of music of past ages in various countries by the great anthologies (*Denkmäler der Tonkunst in Oesterreich, Denkmäler deutscher Tonkunst, Monumenta Musicae Belgicae, Istituzioni e Monumenti dell'Arte Musicale Italiana, Maîtres Musiciens de la Renaissance Française, Musica Britannica,* etc.) and the great editions of the collected works of individual composers for which the original sources are in rare manuscripts or prints.

When scholars first began to make such collections, in the early and middle years of the nineteenth century, they often aimed at "definitive" editions—editions which should decode foreign or obsolete notations and make them fully intelligible to "modern" musicians without any intrusion of the personality of the editor. As the techniques of approaching this goal have been refined it has become increasingly clear that it cannot be reached: that any such translation from one set of symbols to another is an act of interpretation. It involves choosing among possible meanings those which seem likeliest, and among details those which seem most important, to the musicians of the time and place in which the translation is made—and accordingly rejecting others which to musicians of another time and place will seem essential. Accordingly it has been found that the "definitive" editions, such as the Bach-Gesellschaft edition of the Collected Works of Bach, the Breitkopf and Härtel editions of the Collected Works of Mozart and of Palestrina, and the various "Urtext" editions, are inadequate to present-day requirements and must be redone. And while standards of fidelity to the original sources and of accuracy and completeness in conveying their contents in full detail do improve, it is easier for editors of today to realize that their work, in turn, cannot escape being bound to its own time and place.

Awareness of that fact has not acted as the slightest deterrent to new publication of anthologies and collected-works editions. On the contrary, since World War II there has been a new wave of such publications edited by both American and European scholars. Dunstable, Dufay, Ockeghem, Gombert, Clemens non Papa, Walter, Rhaw, Lassus, Bach, Gluck, Mozart, Graupner, Liszt are some of the composers whose collected works have recently been or are in the course of being made available in "scientific" or "critical" editions— editions in which to varying degrees a clear differentiation is made between what has been taken over from the sources and what has been added by the editor. Haydn, on the publication of whose complete works several beginnings have been made, still remains without such representation—the only first-rank composer of the last two hundred years of whom large numbers of works remain inaccessible. The latest attempt is announced as having the support of the West German government, and one may hope that at last this one will succeed. The "Collected Works" of Lassus, perhaps the greatest single figure in the music of the sixteenth century, remain today lamentably incomplete, twenty-nine years after their publication was interrupted; of his fifty-three surviving masses, more than half have never been printed in score.* But these are only two glaring examples. Of the fifteenth, sixteenth, and seventeenth centuries there are hundreds of composers whose names are familiar to us but of whose works we have access to no more than a handful of pieces reprinted in available collections. From these we have no doubt a fragmentary and often distorted view of their composers' significance.

* As this essay goes to press, the first volume of the new series resuming publication of Lassus' complete works has made its appearance.

Would the services of musicology to the practical musician cease if the great bulk of ancient and exotic music were available in notation clear to the performing musician of today? To answer this question one must understand the symbolic and abbreviational character of all graphic notation of music. The contemporary musician would like to think that musical notation is complete, and that from the printed page he can tell exactly how the music would ideally sound. Actually, to the extent that such completeness and accuracy are approached, they are approached only on the basis of tacit assumptions that are far more parochial than is often realized. Yet, since a representative body of recent and contemporary Western music is printed and recorded, often in several versions, there is no reason why future musicians, or representatives of an alien culture, should not be able to form a good idea of the nature of our music and discover most of the unformulated principles upon which it is based.

Since Western musicians first began to seek a graphic notation for their music they have moved almost steadily in the direction of greater and greater minuteness of accuracy in representing the precise duration, pitch, and character of every sound that goes into it. This development, which goes back to the medieval scribes and theorists, received a strong new impetus from Johann Sebastian Bach and his son Emanuel, was advanced particularly by Beethoven, Berlioz, Wagner, and Debussy, and has reached its highest point thus far in the writing of Igor Stravinsky, who, like most contemporary composers, makes his intentions as explicit as possible in every detail, leaving "nothing" to the interpreter's discretion.

But how far this "nothing" is from really nothing, how far even contemporary Western notation stops short of completeness and how much it leaves to the taste, imagination, and intuition of the performer, may be judged in many ways. Why would music critics concern themselves so largely with the qualities of performers as they do, if the performers' only function were to realize the composers' completely defined intentions, like a builder executing an architect's drawings? Why are the "performances" constructed direct from the printed page by engineers on the electronic "synthesizer," theoretically unlimited in its capacities to create every conceivable sound and sound-combination, so ludicrously mechanical in effect?

Contemporary Western notation is undeniably incomplete. But it is the most precise ever used for music, being the culmination of a long process of development such as has hardly even been started in cultures other than our own. And the very fact that contemporary musicians are apt to overestimate its degree of completeness misleads them into imagining that when it is used for musics distant from their own experience in time and place it does—or could, if carefully enough applied—give them a precise idea of such ancient or exotic musics. One need go no further back in time than the eighteenth century, however, and no further afield than jazz or any other popular or folk art, to find music of which the notation, even when it looks exactly like ours, is misleading when read by the modern musician.

This is for two reasons:

1) Many symbols employed before about 1800 had meanings quite different then from the meanings attached to those same symbols today. For example, music teachers nowadays try to teach their students to play "just what is written" and observe the exact proportions between the indicated lengths of different notes. The student is taught to measure exactly the durations of the notes in a rhythmic figure like this

Count: 1   (2   3   4)   2   (2   3   4)   1   (2 3 4)   2   (2 3 4)

by counting aloud at an absolutely even pace. In the eighteenth century, on the other hand, his teacher might have insisted just as firmly on his playing the above notation approximately as we would play something notated as follows:

We ordinarily explain this difference by saying that eighteenth-century music was highly ornamented. It would be more suggestive to the imagination of the modern musician to say that the notation of the eighteenth-century music was highly abbreviated—that the first notation above served as a shorthand for something like the second. The further back we go in music history, the more we encounter such abbreviations and other differences between the meanings attached to symbols in earlier times and in our own, until eventually, of course, many of the symbols themselves are different. One of the principal tasks of musicology has always been to discover what meanings notational symbols had in their own time and to transcribe the music into symbols generally understood at the date of transcription. In this, musicology directly serves, of course, the performing, "practical" musician, making old music available to him in directly singable or playable form.[1]

[1] Sometimes a significant part of the work of ascertaining the original meaning of notation consists in clearing away a mass of "tradition" attaching to the performance of a particular work or type of work.

In the exercise of his interpretative imagination, a great performer, whose playing or singing carries particular conviction, introduces a hastening or slowing down of the tempo, a *sforzato* or a *piano subito*, a *Luftpause* or a *fermata*, that constitutes an integral part of his conception of the piece. Lesser men, then, in search of the secret of the compelling power of the greater artist's interpretation, grasp at the details in which it obviously differs from others—details which the great interpreter has not found explicit in the notation but which have been suggested to him by his own re-creative imagination. And the lesser men imagine that if they imitate these details they will achieve an effect similar to that of the performance in which the details occurred.

Out of these imitations, and imitations of these imitations, are born performance "traditions," which by the time they have earned that im-

2) The relative explicitness and precision of modern Western musical notation reflects a concept in our concert music that is rare in the history and geography of musical cultures: the concept of a musical work as a complete and finished thing which needs only to be "brought to life" or "interpreted" by the performer but in which he must not change and to which he must not add anything on the spur of the moment. Actually, it is only the "notes" that we feel he must not change, by which we really mean the approximate relations of the durations of the notes and their approximate pitches—the two aspects of our music for which our notation is most precise. He must not make a dotted eighth and a sixteenth out of two eighths, or change a C# to a D. These would be the kinds of departure from the graphic notation that we could spot and label definitely a "mistake" or an "unjustifiable liberty." On the whole, the strictness with which we expect the performer to play "just what's written" varies in proportion to the precision with which a particular aspect of our music can be notated and the reading of the notation can be checked by the unaided ear, which means that precision in notation not only reflects but partly also brings about the concept of the complete and finished musical art-work. Thus we have ways of stating the precise speed at which a piece is to go, and even of indicating quite closely rather minute variations in that speed (see, for example, Artur Schnabel's edition of the Beethoven pianoforte sonatas), but we have no easy and convenient way of checking up, in listening, on how closely the performer keeps to the tempo indications. And for degrees of loudness and

pressive name have usually become meaningless distortions guarded with opinionated obstinacy and a sort of guild or secret-society pedantry by those who have no conception of how they arose or what purpose they originally served. Probably few of them have any connection with the composer. Whatever their origin, the musicologist must help the practical musician to free himself from any supposed obligations imposed by them, and thus to make his own direct contact with the notation in which the composer has symbolized his intention and arrive at his own independent understanding of its meaning.

nuances of tone color even the indications are not precise.
Accordingly we do not expect nearly such literal adherence
on the part of the performer to the symbols indicating speed,
loudness, or tone-color, as to those indicating pitch and relative duration. These less precisely notated (or notatable)
factors we say belong to the performer's "interpretation."

In most musical cultures other than our own there is no
such concept as that of the complete and finished composition, and it is recent even in our own culture. In most musics,
a "composition" embodies a group of ideas, melodic, rhythmic, structural, which serve the performer—who is originally
always the composer himself—as a basis for more or less wide-
ranging improvisatory elaboration. Here, a piece of music is
never the same twice. Even if on occasion it is performed in
such a way that it could be notated in our symbols with a
fair approximation to precision, there is no one authentic
version that can or should be committed to paper as "the
piece."

Western musicians of today have such strong habits of
associating a piece of music with its graphic notation that
they need constant reminding, by every possible means, of
the limitations of notation as applied to either old or exotic
music. The hunt for *the authentic version* of a piece by even
so recent a composer as J. S. Bach (1685-1750), though one of
the principal preoccupations of beginners in musicological
interest, and the task that many "practical musicians" expect
of musicologists, is a vain one. Neither Bach nor any other
good musician up to at least Bach's time probably ever played
a piece exactly the same way twice. And by "the same way"
we mean here nothing so narrow as the musician of today
may understand. We mean that he probably never played
exactly the same notes twice, or played them in exactly the
same rhythm.

Improvisation and performance are normally, one may say,
inseparable. It is only in the unique cultural and social
situation of Western music since about 1800 that they have
become divorced. Consequently, only the Western musician

since about 1800 has been liable to the misunderstanding which attributes to all musical notations, and to transcriptions into modern Western notation of music of earlier times or alien cultures, a precision which is applicable only to the music of this one part of the world in this one corner of history.

The true task of musicology is of course to learn as much as it can about music itself. To the extent that notations or transcriptions represent abstractions which leave out a great deal that belongs, or belonged, to the living music, musicology must try to recapture what has been left out, or at the very least form an opinion on what sort of thing it was. Its task only begins with the setting up of clear, "authoritative" texts. What it must really teach the practical musician is what lies behind and around those texts, what tacit assumptions originally clothed with the flesh of music the bare bones that survive for preservation in scholarly editions.

It is no accident that what this means is the reuniting of the "musicological" relics conserved in scholarly editions with the *musical practice* from which they derive. Music is something people do. Musicology must always be concerned with what they do in the particular music under study and how they do it—that is, with practical musicianship. Similarly, musical performance, while it must be guided by intuition, needs also, if it is to be something more than pure *Ausdruck der Empfindung,* to partake of musicology. The two activities—performance and scholarly investigation—are aspects of the same search. The musicologist cannot fruitfully inquire into the nature of music if by his own lack of musicality he forgets what it is or is debarred from knowing. The performer cannot present or "interpret" anyone else's music to any greater extent than he himself understands it.

How does musicology in practice proceed, having exhumed the bones of ancient music, to put back on them the flesh of living music? It is more and more widely agreed that the bones need not be presented in editions so ostentatiously scholarly that only scholars can use them. For primary scholarly investigation, nothing can take the place of facsimile reproduction of original sources. For quicker inspection, musical scholars like other musicians need a presentation of the music that is as easy to read as it can be made, while always differentiating so clearly between what has been done by the editor and what has been taken over from the original sources that it would be possible to reconstruct the sources from the edition. Such an edition is not easy to make. Like every other editor, I believe that there are ways in which our techniques of representing old or exotic music could be improved. But once one has admitted to oneself that any edition is an interpretation, and that it is the editor's job to present the music in such fashion that the reader will know both what the editor found in the sources and what he thinks it means, the job is not impossible. Publications like Apel's anthology of music from fourteenth-century France or Kirkpatrick's edition of Bach's *Goldberg Variations* exemplify the best in such techniques.[2] In making available works that have been inaccessible to the public for centuries, or a corpus of exotic music that has never been published, one should assume that in all probability this music will not be published again for a long time, and the new publication should wherever possible (it is rarely impossible) serve the needs of both scholars and practical performers. There is no better way of encouraging both within their limitations to be both.

There is often more that the editor should tell the reader

[2] In the case of composers whose notation and point of view are far removed from ours, it would be possible and perhaps desirable to make new editions which would differ widely from the existing ones so far as editorial interpretation goes—along the lines suggested by the late Otto Gombosi, for example—but would still make clear how the original sources read. Gombosi's ideas of how music of the 14th- to 16th-centuries was organized, and how it should sound, were different from the traditional notions. Such ideas contribute to our understanding, and have a right to be represented in print, so long as they are conveyed in a way which makes clear the nature of the sources they interpret,

about what this music meant—how it was performed, used, listened to in its own time and place—than can be embodied in the notation itself, sometimes more than can even be printed in the prefatory matter and annotations. Then it becomes the editor's task to write about it in separate books or articles—such books and articles as are too few and far between. There is a good deal of writing about the history of performance, but the subject is hard to treat without straying to one side or the other of the ideal path. Such writing should, like editing, fulfill two requirements. It should present the editor's considered view of the problems and their solution; and it should marshal, in a form that clearly differentiates it from the editor's inferences, conclusions, and judgments, the evidence on which that view is based. When this is done, the reader has a guide through what otherwise might be an impenetrable forest of evidence, but he knows when he is being guided and when he is finding his way with his own eyes. Even guides with somewhat extremist views (like Dolmetsch or Schering, to the considerable extent that they observe both of these requirements) will not for long mislead the serious student, who can see when they are arguing from the evidence and when they are stretching it to suit their *partis pris*. On the other hand, even such balanced and sensible writings as Thurston Dart's *Interpretation of Music* and Tovey's introductions to his Bach and Beethoven editions, although the informed reader will more often than not agree with their conclusions, are dangerous leaders. For they often give the uninformed exactly what they tend to look for: the conclusions in all too handy form, without the necessity or the opportunity of considering the evidence on which they are based.

And this brings us to one of the realities of the situation. Musicology, we have said, must be concerned with what musicians do and how they do it. It must also be somewhat concerned with what they do not do. Now what many of the most influential performing musicians do not do is read, and what they particularly do not read is musicology. They distrust, not always without reason, what they have sometimes referred to as "words without music."

The language performing musicians understand best is music performed, or notated in such detail that lying still on the page it is half-performed. Scholars, to teach people what the music printed in their scholarly editions means, must get that music performed (and in these days preferably recorded) as they think it should be, which means almost always that they themselves must perform it or at least direct its performance. That, too, is the best way they can find out what notation means to performers, and therefore how one should notate in order to convey to a performing musician a given intention. In this way the scholar's own performance becomes not only a means of conveying his ideas, but a tool in his research. Once more one sees the inevitability and desirability of a *rapprochement* between musicology and practical musicianship.

The musicologist must know how musicians have thought, and a principal clue to this, though it needs to be used with discretion, is how musicians think today. The practical musician is apt to remain uninterested in musical research or its results until they are demonstrated to him in sound. When, however, one does approach him verbally, it is certainly most effective to guide him to the evidence and help him learn to judge it for himself rather than feed him a predigested version of it. The latter he is apt to take as the Law and the Prophets, so that when he encounters a different version, issuing from what may seem to him equally good authority, he will fall from naive optimism into naive pessimism, and feel that he has good ground for thinking that scholars never know what they are talking about and the only sure guide is his artistic instinct.

And of course artistic instinct, though not an infallible guide, is an indispensable one, not only for the performer but for the musical scholar. In the documentary evidence, the scholar frequently comes upon material that contradicts his expectations and presents the musical practice he is investigating in a new light, unfamiliar and, at first at least, unconvincing to his feelings for the music. If he has any real bent, he cannot instantaneously change those feelings from datum to new datum. At times he must even present his findings before he has reconciled himself to some of their contents. To indulge in the sort of casuistry that fools himself and some of his readers is a temptation that musicologists have not always resisted. But the man who is more interested in knowing than in seeming to know will not accept an apparent fact that goes against his grain, or gloss it over like an oyster making a pearl. He will work with it—try the experiment of acting as if it were true—until he either succeeds in finding it no longer repugnant and in assimilating it, or discovers further data which put the refractory one in its place, or frankly admits that although it is among the evidence he has found he does not know what to make of it, and cannot accept it at face value. If it concerns performance —the rhythm or tempo of a piece, say; or the ornamentation of a line; or a feature of instrumental or vocal technique— he will try it out repeatedly, or persuade a musician better qualified than himself to give it an adequate trial, and if he cannot accept it wholeheartedly he cannot recommend it without reservation to others, even though the documents seem to prove its validity.[3]

3 An example of the sort of refractory data I mean is the ornament which Giulio Caccini, in the introduction to his *Nuove Musiche* calls *Trillo*. He notates it—

and explains that "the trill described by me is upon one note only." His instructions are "to begin with the first crotchet and to beat every note with the throat upon the vowel 'a' unto the last breve. . . ." Playford, in printing a translation of this passage, quotes a gentleman who "used this grace very exactly" as saying: "I used at my first learning the trill to indicate that breaking of the sound in the throat which men use when they lure their hawks, as *he-he-he-he-he*." If this means what it

Musicology, then, performs valuable services for the practical musician, and can do so best when the musicologist and the practical musician are in closest *rapport* and partake to a considerable extent of each other's qualities.

But it would be a distorted view to look upon musicology as exclusively or primarily the servant of the practical mu-

---

seems to mean, viz., that the continuity of the tone was continually interrupted by actual aspirations or glottal stops, the technique of producing this ornament has disappeared, and when one attempts to revive it the effect is (initially, at least) ludicrous. Tosi, in 1723, made fun of the "prodigious Art of singing like a Cricket." It is tempting to dismiss the whole thing as only a clumsy attempt on Caccini's part to describe the singer's vibrato or tremolo. Unless one has heard or produced the interrupted tone Caccini and Playford seem to describe, one cannot pretend to be sure that it existed; but neither can one be perfectly sure that it did not. My "instinct," which may well be mistaken, leads me to think they meant a controlled vibrato. So, while I would encourage any singer to experiment and see if he can produce a continually interrupted tone that he and I can learn to find ornamental, until he succeeds in doing so I could not honestly try to persuade him that he must take Caccini's and Playford's explanations at face value.

Musica ficta—the application of "understood" accidentals to supplement those that are explicit in the sources of medieval and Renaissance music—is another field in which scholars ought to be aware and make their readers aware of the extent to which they are guided by instinct. Clear differentiation between the accidentals found in the sources and those the editor suggests as properly to be added is an obligation widely recognized. But the fact that the suggested accidentals are to be printed in brackets, or above the notes instead of next to them, does not relieve the editor of the duty of trying to give his suggestions a certain consistency among themselves, and of stating as explicitly as possible the principles determining that consistency. Three basic attitudes are possible: (1) that the accidentals in the sources are self-sufficient; (2) that more or less definite general principles for supplementing the explicit accidentals were systematically applied in performance and should be applied in editing; (3) that the application of these principles was to a considerable extent a matter for the discretion and taste of the musician in charge of each performance. Our knowledge of this subject is today not sufficiently well organized to remove this question from those that must be decided partly by instinct. Indeed the subject provides a sort of model example of both the indispensability of artistic instinct as a scholarly tool and the dangers of overreliance upon it.

sician. The practical musician seeks above all the completest understanding, more intuitive than intellectual, of one work at a time. Without such intuitive understanding of individual works the musicologist, too, would be lost, for he cannot hope to understand the relations between works if he does not understand the works themselves. And the understanding of a work of art is by definition a matter of feeling as well as of thought. But beyond the individual art-work, the musicologist wants to understand its relations with other works—works by the same composer and other composers, in the same time and in other times—and the techniques, forms, styles, intellectual and spiritual currents it represents. The practical musician, *qua* practical musician, is interested in such broader questions only to the extent that they illuminate the individual work for him. The musicologist— since to be a competent musicologist he must be to some extent a practical musician, too—cannot take the diametrically opposed view. But *qua* historian or musical anthropologist he is interested in the individual work only to the extent that it contributes to his understanding of developments and relationships.

Accordingly, a work that interests the musicologist greatly may be of no interest to the practical musician. The link between one phenomenon and another may be of surpassing historical or systematic interest, but its "absolute" aesthetic value is sometimes less than either of the things it connects. Musicologists often feel called upon to claim an "intrinsic" value in music whose chief interest for them actually, and quite legitimately, lies in its historic, not its aesthetic, importance. To make such a claim is a mistake. It confuses the issues, and it places the case for publishing and studying this music on the wrong basis, and often on a weak one. The general historian does not feel called upon to claim intrinsic worth for the men or absolute value for the events he studies. It should be recognized that to understand the history of music the musicologist must study and publish much music that is in itself of little value to the practical musician—music that he would not, if he is a sensible man, recommend to the practical musician as material for performance, however significant it may be from a historical point of view. To understand it himself, the musicologist must try to perform it or get it performed, with as close an approach as possible to the attitude and artistic conviction which gave it birth and with which it was originally performed. For music itself, not just the black and white abstraction of it, is the object of his study. But such performance is a laboratory experiment, the success of which is in no way to be measured by the aesthetic value of the music performed.

Musicology renders important services to the practical musician, who is one of its most important and in some ways most congenial clients. But the subject of music history is history, and the subject of ethnomusicology is exotic cultures—as well as music. The purpose of musicology is the increase of understanding: for the general historian; for the historian of art, of language, of thought, of culture; for the ethnologist and the anthropologist; for the psychologist, the semanticist, and the critic; and for the practical musician. And if it is the practical musician who is the most direct beneficiary, a basic factor in determining the value of the musicological research upon which he draws will always be the extent to which it maintains its integrity as an independent field of inquiry, a pure science, making its contribution to man's understanding of himself, and leaving it to anyone to turn that understanding to his own best account.

The Lore of Non-Western Music

By CURT SACHS

THE LORE OF NON-WESTERN MUSIC

The Confucian *Analects* report how in ancient China, almost six hundred years B.C., a group of pretty slave girls from Ch'i arrived at the palace of Chi Huan and how court was suspended for three days to enjoy their unaccustomed music. Whereupon Confucius, who was attending court, withdrew in disapproval—a protest of the mind against the senses.

The dissent of the wise philosopher is the only unusual fact in this story; the importation and popularity of foreign girl-musicians were characteristic of all ancient civilizations. In India, the Greek geographer Strabo tells us, an effective means of buying the favors of influential rajahs was a present of attractive singing girls from Alexandria or Palestine, and Eudoxios of Cadiz in Spain shipped women trained in music to India as part of his trade; Arabian courts entertained Hellenic girl-musicians; the Egyptian princess whom King Solomon took for wife, so the Talmud relates, brought a thousand musical instruments in her dowry, and we may boldly assume that she had the necessary players in her retinue; in Egypt itself, a mural in King Amenophis IV's capital—the oldest pertinent document—shows the Pharaoh's singing girls from Syria practicing their art in a roofless house.

Beautiful women with musical training were a typical gift to royal friends or suzerains all over the ancient world from Egypt to China. These women carried art to the East and the West, charming the educated elite with the irresistible appeal of dancing, music, poetry, and sex, and adding to this appeal the flavor of exoticism.

But enjoyment was not the only result of this transcontinental and transoceanic exchange. Besides affording delight and excitement, the singing girls became exporters who, dis-

21

regarding the frontiers of countries and races, made known the styles from far away. They did not, however, create a cosmopolitan idiom; nor should one misconceive their international role, for their influence was limited to courtly circles. But, as they widened the horizons of native musicians, they stimulated comparison which acted as a ferment to keep the national styles from stagnation.

The desire for music from abroad was especially strong and well fulfilled in China, even though the element of feminine attractiveness was absent. From antiquity right up to the recent end of the monarchy, the imperial court harbored not only domestic bands and orchestras but also foreign orchestras imported from Korea, Japan, Indochina, and Burma, from India, Turkistan, Mongolia, and other countries, in short, from almost everywhere in Asia. These orchestras were evidently never meant to be a kind of museum in sound, representing Asiatic music. Rather they were a proud display of might. In many cases the countries whence the musicians were drawn were parts of the empire, in others allies of the empire. The orchestras were, in some cases, peaceful presents, in others tributes reluctantly offered, in still others, spoils of war and conquest, or again the live dowries of foreign princesses. Yet the musical point of view was not altogether ignored: we are told, for example, that in 605 A.D. a Cambodian group that had been unfavorably received was sent back home.

These organized ensembles, however, form only one part of the picture. Individual musicians have for thousands of years journeyed, voluntarily or under duress, on sailing vessels across the sea or by caravan routes across the land, to display their art in the exalted atmosphere of faraway palaces or in the humbler surroundings of crowded, turbulent seaports. Musicians, like tradesmen, have always become travelers, once they no longer have a share in the economy of the village, in fishing and hunting, in herding or tilling the soil, or in applying the practical crafts of the community. But, although uprooted and homeless, they are still tied to their people by the musical language they speak, the rhythms and nostalgic tunes they play and sing.

This is also true of the individual slaves, who were so essential a part of ancient life. And again, as with the orchestras, it is the girl well trained in music who had the greatest chance of being sold to play and sing for a lady of social standing or to brighten the monotonous seclusion of harem life. Plato mentions this musical role in the passage in which he cautions his fellow citizens against the Asiatic harps of Oriental slave girls in Athenian houses: the harp, he warns, yields too readily and therefore endangers the austerity that should mark the music of the Greeks. Here, then, is evidence that foreign music had a shaping power; the national heritage may have been strong everywhere, but it did not stay unchallenged.

But even without the strumming slaves, Greece had an Oriental, or at least an East-born, music. This would be a bold assertion but for the convincing statement of Strabo. The learned geographer tells us that his nation had taken all its music from Asia. Even the names of instruments, like *lyra, kithara, phorminx,* or *syrinx, aulos, salpinx,* are conspicuously un-Hellenic. In time, it is true, Greek music won an identity of its own; but the process must have taken centuries to unfold.

The fact itself is clear enough. Again and again, conquering tribes of a militarily superior but culturally inferior type have fallen captive to the more advanced civilization of the conquered lands. The same adaptation occurs when neighboring cultures struggle with one another over a protracted period of time. Take the Dorian Greeks, who before 1000 B.C. swept down from the Danube basin, overran Mycenae and Crete, and learned both music and dancing from the Cretans. Take the Vedic Aryas, who accepted the music and the visual arts of culturally superior India after conquering the northern half of the subcontinent. Take the New Kingdom of Egypt which, holding Southwest Asia in thrall, adopted much of the music of the vanquished, as is shown not only by the presence of slave girls, already mentioned, but also by the sudden influx of Asiatic instruments, of lyres, lutes, oboes, drums, and castanets. Take Arabia, which formed her music out of the musical treasures of Persia, Turkey, Syria, and Egypt when she carried the Koran west to Spain and east to Java.

This rule, almost a law, that culture seeps down from above, explains the origin and early fate of Western music. Judged from what we see and are able to interpret, the musical heritage of northern, central, and western Europe before 1000 A.D. was much less significant than we are inclined to assume. True, folksong must have existed, and we can even infer that, in the building of northern melodies, certain characteristic traits resisted all influences from the south—such traits, for example, as the preference for the third over the fourth, which was favored along the shores of the Mediterranean. But there is not the slightest trace of art music, of a musical system, of notation, or of any set of rules beyond the oral tradition of primitive tribes. This barbarian world yielded ground when it felt the impact of two formidable powers exerting pressure from the south.

One of these was the Church. Its thousands of melodies, Mediterranean in style and origin, crystallized around a Hebrew kernel; and its peculiar singing, florid in comparison with the sober matching of one note to a syllable, usual in northern folksongs, penetrated early to transalpine countries in company with the Christian faith and ritual. These melodies became compulsory about the year 600, when Pope Gregory I enforced their use, to the exclusion of other melodies, in every church of the Western, or Roman, creed. How violent the impact of this Mediterranean intrusion was, cannot easily be overestimated. It was the more sweeping, as this, the earliest regular and systematized music to spread north from the Mediterranean, prompted serious attempts on the part of erudite monks to create a solid theoretical foundation with the help of Roman and Arabic sources. The Gregorian melodies are sung in Catholic churches to this day; they permeated religious and secular composition in the Middle Ages and later periods; and they appear in many scores of the twentieth century.

The other great southern power making itself felt in Italy, Sicily, and Spain was Islamic civilization. During the almost eight hundred years of its sway, Europe could boast nothing to match the refined musical culture of such Arabian and Moorish centers as Cordova, Seville, and Granada. Once more, the inferior civilization yielded to the higher; and, in spite of permanent war and hostility, Oriental music was cherished at Christian courts and slowly advanced northward and eastward. As late as the sixteenth century, long after the Muslims had left the Iberian peninsula, the Spaniards still sang one of their famous songs with its Arabic text and undoubtedly with its Arabic melody.

But we need not dwell on such isolated bits of evidence. To see the enormous range of the Muhammedan influx, we should note the astonishing fact that among the many instruments used in medieval Europe not a single one was indigenous. A few had come from the Byzantine Orient: the organ, the fiddle (the precursor of our modern violin), and the bell chime. All the others came from Islamic Spain: the citterns, lutes, guitars, and their kin, the multiform zithers, struck or plucked, the various families of oboes, trumpets, and drums. True, these were later perfected by European makers, and the zithers—dulcimer and psaltery—were provided with keyboards when Western polyphony required the simultaneous playing of several voice parts. But they had come from the East, and for a long time the Europeans called them by their Arabic names—*añafil, atabal, cañon, rabé*. One of these instruments almost preserved its original name: "lute" is the Arabic *al 'ūd,* "the wood."

More curious is the tenacity with which the bagpipe has clung to its distinctly Arabian scale with whole tones and three-quarter tones in the midst of a world of diatonic scales. Wherever the old Oriental instrument appears on its journey to Scotland—in the Mediterranean, Spain, or Brittany—the foreign scale is preserved; and it is quite an experience to watch the guards march into Buckingham Palace, the band playing "correctly" and the bagpipers "in Arabic."

Oriental influence in the Middle Ages was èvidently not limited to the instruments, and not even to their particular scales: no instrument travels without its music. The medieval melodies that we see on paper, the archaic quadrangular notes so neatly written on staff lines or in the spaces between, look innocently diatonic and European—just as do the native melodies that modern Orientals try to write down in Western notation. But were those medieval melodies actually sung as they sound when played on an equal-tempered piano? Hardly. Give them the many unwritable shades of Arabian intervals from note to note, now a little wider, now narrower than ours, try to give them the color, the intonation, the strange mannerisms of Oriental singing, and the whole illusion of Western style is gone.

This is not a fanciful interpretation. One can still watch how the Spanish *Flamenco,* whatever its homeland and origin, is carefully studied by those who want to sing it, not only with regard to the melodic succession, but above all with regard to the exact, unalterable rendering that oral tradition has faithfully preserved through nobody knows how many hundreds or thousands of years. Our notes deceive us: performance style, which they cannot express, counts for more than the bald arrangement of steps that they set forth. How dare we suppose that the Christian Spaniards and Provençals sheared the Moorish melodies of all their characteristic traits! Incidentally, one picture, and a very late one, provides a strange confirmation: in the famous altarpiece of Ghent (*c.* 1425, that is, in the time of Dufay), van Eyck painted the singing angels grouped around St. Cecilia with, above the nose, the quite un-European but typically Oriental creases which result from nasal singing and which we find so often five thousand years ago in the portraits of Egyptian singers and in the living Orient of today. (Commercial photos of the altar seldom show this detail.)

Time and again, an Oriental word, an Oriental idea crops up in medieval treatises and testifies to the arduous studies of Arabic sources. One anonymous writer uses the corrupt Arabic words *elmuahym* and *elmuarifa* as musical terms. Another author mentions the word *scambs*, which despite its cryptic spelling is nothing else than Arabic *shams* or "sun," corresponding to its Latin synonym *sol,* the symbol and name of the note G.

Sol begot the name solmization, which stands for a method, still in use, of memorizing a melody by giving each note a syllable to be sung instead of a text—*ut* (or *do*) *re mi fa sol la.* Such solmization systems were known in India, ancient Greece, and the Muslim countries long before they came to be known in Europe in the Middle Ages. And the same is true of the "Guidonian hand," attributed to the monk Guido of Arezzo in the eleventh century, on which every note had a corresponding fixed place that was to be touched with the index finger of the right hand for the purpose of adding tactile to aural and visual memory.

But above all we are indebted to the ancient Orient for our musical script. As a system of "neumes," it had been a set of symbols for entire groups of steps—up-down, up-down-up, down-up-down, and so forth—without being concerned with pitches, and hence it was quite appropriate for the latitude given to the steps of Oriental (and probably Occidental medieval) melodies. It was from these dashes, dots, and hooks that the Europeans developed our staff notation by a long, laborious evolution.

Only Europe's turning to polyphony and harmony severed the numerous ties between the East and the West. The music of the Renaissance, in the hundred years before and after 1500, was nearly self-sufficient. Engrossed in the "vertical" relations of simultaneous notes and voice parts, it had nothing to learn from the "horizontal" expanse of Eastern melody.

The new relations were at first of little significance and rather peripheral. They had been prepared long ago in a field quite strictly separated from "regular" music: in the fifteenth century, the Hungarians had introduced from India and the Islamic countries the big kettledrums played on horseback to accompany the trumpets of princes and their cavalry regiments. Far from sensing the later musical importance of timpani, contemporaries complained bitterly. "These are enormous rumbling barrels. They trouble honest old people, the ill and the sick, the devout in monasteries who study, read, and pray; and I think and believe that the devil has invented and made them."

A new East-West connection through percussion music derived indirectly from the conquest of Constantinople and the consequent advance of the Turks westward across the Balkan Peninsula, which became a threat to the Continent. For two hundred and fifty years, their noisy bands of shrieking shawms and wild percussion spurred on the Turkish soldiers in march and battle; during two hundred and fifty years they terrified the southeast of Europe. At last the Turkish armies were routed by Prince Eugene (1716-17). Many of their instruments were captured and used as sounding symbols of victory. More and more European regiments— as far west as France—adopted Turkish percussion: bass drums, cymbals, triangle, and the jingling crescent with its dangling Ottoman horsetails. More and more, too, this so-called Turkish music, but without the crescent, conquered the orchestras of concert hall and opera house. At first these percussion effects were merely characteristic, evoking march, parade and combat, as in Haydn's Military Symphony (1794). Soon, however, the Turkish music was dissolved into its components and individually merged with the orchestra. Thus Gluck used wild-clashing cymbals to flavor the barbarian choruses in his Tauridian Iphigenia, and Beethoven called upon the triangle to add inimitable zest and energy to the last movement of the Ninth.

Turkey, no longer terrifying, became comic in the inevitable reaction against fright, like the fairy tale ogre or the blinded Polyphemus of Homeric legend. As a result, the *opera buffa* of the eighteenth century often displayed some Turkish background, from Gluck's *Rencontre imprévue* to Mozart's *Entführung aus dem Serail*. We should look vainly, however, for Turkish or Arabian music in these scores, or even in Mozart's well-known *Rondo alla turca*. Eighteenth-century composers were content with what they imagined Oriental music to be; they did not present it as it actually was. The Oriental flavor came from Austrian kitchens, not from the spice stalls of an Istanbul bazaar.

This short report must close with the most curious of all Turkicisms: early in the nineteenth century south German manufacturers produced (by no means as something exceptional) upright pianos with an additional pedal, which enabled a player to strike a triangle or cymbals and even to pound the sounding board with a bass drum stick.

The turn to more authentic Oriental expression, albeit in a narrower sense, occurred with the Romanticism of the early nineteenth century. With eyes and ears alert to everything characteristic or peculiar, the public developed a new attitude. Pseudo-orientalism, marked at best by a bit of percussion here and there, was no longer acceptable. When Carl Maria von Weber wrote his overture to Schiller's adaptation of Gozzi's *Turandot,* he copied a genuine Chinese melody from Jean-Jacques Rousseau's *Dictionnaire de musique* of 1768. Almost a generation later (1844) Félicien David composed the symphonic ode, *Le Désert,* which—like the paintings of his contemporary, Eugène Delacroix—took its inspiration from actual travels and studies in Oriental lands. His Orientalism, drawn from neither books nor imagination, was based on direct experience.

Such a list could easily be continued over the succeeding hundred years, down to Busoni's (American) *Indian Diary* or Henry Cowell's Java-inspired works. Nor must we forget Debussy who, though far from writing Oriental music, nevertheless appropriated his famous whole-tone scale from the music of a Javanese orchestra appearing at the World Fair in Paris. Here, then, we finally return to that Oriental music which penetrated European art as a shaping force, not merely as a decorative factor.

This return resulted from the critical position Western music had reached, a position marked by an extraordinary increase of sensitiveness and receptivity. On the one hand Wagner's *Tristan* had irrevocably dissolved the restrictive dualism of major and minor; on the other hand the young Frenchmen and Italians shunned the opaque grandiloquence of the neo-Germans and of Classicism and Romanticism as well. The foundations of the nineteenth century were shaken, and the world awaited something new. The people of the West no longer listened to Oriental music with a certain degree of superciliousness, but with the humble eagerness of less prejudiced minds. Indicative of the change was the little-known pioneer, Louis-Albert Bourgault-Ducoudray of Paris, who published in 1876 thirty Greek and Oriental melodies. In his preface he stated that he hoped "to widen the horizon among the musicians of Europe."

Feeling the impact of Oriental music, a few persons began to realize that Western music was not unlimited. It dawned upon some musicologists, perhaps for the first time, that our great achievements in harmony, polyphony, and orchestration had involved sacrifices in other fields; that Europe had compressed into the conventional major and minor the incredible richness of melodic types and modes that still flourished in the East; that the West's even, unalterable semitones, forced into a uniform "equal temperament," had supplanted a wealth of variable tunings. Under the strait jacket of harmonic motion our melody had become a poor device connecting related chords, while Western rhythm, its counterpart infinitely subtle in the East, had degenerated into a system that did little more than mark binary or ternary accent groups.

It was a wholesome shock, actually stronger in America

than in Europe, to realize that the antithesis of our glorious Western music was not simply the primitive babble of less advanced peoples. America's acceptance of more than conventional music is far-reaching. Her modern Russian and Negro music connects, though indirectly, with the Orient. The Russians and the Negroes, through many hundreds of years, have absorbed the influx of Oriental music; and both of these peoples have quickened in us an innate sense of motor impulse and melodic freedom.

This new approach to the Orient, conscious or unconscious, signifies neither a cheap imitation of foreign wares nor a belittling of the great traditions of our Western world. It points, rather, to a widening of the resources of art, to the reconquest of lost but valuable ground which the white man has long since forgotten. It brings us to a music which the East has faithfully preserved and kept alive. In this sense, and in no other, do we find our musical exoticism.

The word "exoticism," shorn of its "ism" and Greek solemnity, covers our interest in men and things located in other, different civilizations. This interest springs from urges inherent in the transitional phases of our cultural cycles—urges to become centrifugal and centripetal; to master the world, not by conquering but by absorbing it; to accept difference, even to enjoy it, as a complement to our own limitations. There is an urge, in fact, felt in the final phases of cultural cycles, that leads to naturalism, that prefers character to beauty, that favors life as it is (vital, warm, even repulsive) over the frozen ideals having no connection with the world. Thus the sculpture of Greece, whether in archaic times or in the Golden Age of Pericles, displayed neither exoticism nor naturalism. But in the glowing sunset of Hellenism, artists readily presented a fat old woman in all her repugnant nakedness, or a deformed dancer entertaining banquet guests, or a Trojan priest and his two sons being choked to death in the coils of serpents. Just as readily did these artists depict barbarians from Gaul and Africa. Exoticism and naturalism have this in common: they both oppose frigid academicism and its soulless classical paragons.

The end of the nineteenth century provided an ideal arena for such a clash. Naturalism—the rendering of life as it is, not as we wish it to be—reigned supreme in novels and plays: Flaubert and Zola, Dostoevski and Gorki, Ibsen and Strindberg reveal the sick and the poor, the sinner, the victims of heredity and society, and human frailty in general. Painters and sculptors avoid the frosty canon of flawless beauty and conventional pose. They depict the life of the destitute, and portray the faces of grief and despair. Musical dramatists—the Puccinis, Mascagnis, Leoncavallos, and Charpentiers—turn their backs on spear-shaking gods and make themselves at home in the here and now of "verism."

It was in the year of Charpentier's *Louise,* so belligerently entitled a *"roman musical,"* that Judith Gautier devoted a portly volume of *Musiques bizarres* to the exotic sections of the World's Fair in Paris.

The attitudes of Western man toward Eastern music, as far as we have reviewed them, have a common characteristic. When the ancient world exchanged its singing slaves, when Greece and the Middle Ages fed on Oriental music, when the recent past gave renewed attention to Asiatic rhythms and scales, the interest was always personal and possessive. It led to questions like these: What does this music mean to me? Can I enjoy it? What do we learn, what can we take from it to improve our own music or, at least, to evoke a picture of the East when occasion calls for it?

This possessive attitude is, of course, egocentric, reflexive. The pronouns *I* and *we, my* and *our* govern its pronunciamentos.

Everyone assumes this attitude. Everyone feels it his right to select paintings for his house according to his personal taste, or to hasten through the art museum wing that bores him. Everyone refuses to play a piece he finds unsympathetic, or to attend a concert of music he dislikes. The *rapport* of art and personal taste is proper and natural, and it remains so, even when taste forsakes the orbit of personal self and lodges in the collective ego of an entire cultural sphere. Thus the Italian Renaissance, unbelievably wrapped up in itself and its ancient progenitors, could appreciate no art that followed divergent principles. It stigmatized the cathedral style of the High Middle Ages by the term Gothic, that is, "barbarian," and it claimed that no music earlier than 1430 deserved a hearing. We can take a step further and say that, without such discrimination and collective rejection, no evolution, no change of style would ever occur.

Fortunately such an egocentric attitude, admittedly proper and natural, is not the only possible line of behavior.

By way of example let us think of excavations in Egypt, Babylonia, or Central America. The Renaissance, it is true, had also turned the soil, but chiefly to find Roman objects, columns and torsos which, to fifteenth-century Italy, were ideal standards for architecture and sculpture. These excavations, therefore, served only selfish utilitarian ends.

The subsequent excavations were different. The temples of the Nile were, to be sure, foreign to the Rome-inspired canons of Western architecture, likewise their statues and murals. Excavating was now done for its own sake, not for aesthetic delight or to encourage imitation in the modern West. No one would dream of erecting a sham palace of Rameses in Times Square or on Capitol Hill.

The stimulus behind all recent excavations in Africa, Asia, or America is curiosity, the precious curiosity of the scholar who, literally, leaves no stone unturned in order to wrest the hidden secrets from past civilizations, the older the better. And accompanying this curiosity—the mother of knowledge and insight—is an insatiable pleasure in artistic expressions remote from ours, yet convincing and human; in expressions deviating from the principles we deem necessary. These expressions may seem opposed to ours, differing from our traditions, beliefs, and ideals, yet they are, in their own right, irresistibly alluring.

This situation suggests a new level of culture. The conventional query of the past, "Does this art meet my demands and expectations?" must yield to its opposite, "Do I meet the requirements of this art?"

The meeting of these requirements demands somewhat more than an open eye for art. We must seek to understand not only the foreign art itself, with its achievements and its shortcomings, but also the mind and culture that it expresses and from which it cannot be separated. This implies a talent for empathy, for self-projection into alien and seemingly odd phenomena. Such understanding requires a free and elastic mind and a wholehearted devotion to research; it rests upon the broadminded teachings of modern anthropology. We cannot dismiss, deride, or despise those human beings who differ from us; we have to understand them and, in so doing, understand better ourselves and our own position in the world and in history. What we all too lightly call understanding is, in fact, the inspiring, essential awareness of a meaningful order—and we ourselves are part of it.

A civilization developing from naive egocentricity to such enlightened awareness cannot long ignore the importance of music.

Music imposes, however, enormous difficulties. Our eyes are more tolerant, more adaptable than our ears; we render justice more easily to visual than to aural surprises; and we find representative or illustrative art more accessible than nonrepresentative, "absolute" music.

Moreover, where is the music of Egypt, Babylonia, or Central America? The monuments stand—the music has vanished. No script tells us what the music was like in millennia B.C. Even though a number of symbols exist that may, probably do, represent a musical notation, we are not now and undoubtedly never shall be able to decipher them, to reconstruct a music that seems to be irretrievably lost. A musical picture, frustratingly vague, can be assembled only from the recognizable potentialities of musical instruments found by the excavators of ancient tombs or from the murals and reliefs executed by ancient artists. Occasionally some help comes from hieroglyphic or cuneiform inscriptions, but these are scarce and obscure. So we must, finally, "project backwards" what we know of the most archaic music still to be heard in the lands of excavation and be grateful for the often unbelievable tenacity of Eastern music.

A road to the past of music was opened long before the time of excavations. The background of older European education, partly theological, partly classical, demanded that historical writings on music be prefaced by a reverent bow to Hebrews and Greeks, to Miriam and King David, to Pythagoras and Boethius. The music of the Bible was lost; the few relics of Greek music known today were not yet re-discovered. But authors practiced the intricate art of drawing from literary sources, from biblical passages, and from the plentiful extant works of Hellenic philosophers, poets, and scientists.

The first volume of Padre Martini's *Storia della musica* (1757), its three tomes not progressing beyond antiquity, was devoted to the Hebrews "dalla Creazione d'Adamo" to the Chaldeans and "altri Popoli Orientali" and the Egyptians. The new Oriental archeology of the excavators had found its musical, albeit less glamorous, counterpart. This was followed by the two monumental works of Burney and Hawkins. The first volume of Charles Burney's *General History of Music* (1776) concerned itself with no Chaldeans or other Oriental peoples, but it opened its discussions at least with a sizeable chapter on Egyptian music. Sir John Hawkins, in his *General History of the Science and Practice of Music* (also 1776), while ignoring the Egyptians, allotted some three hundred pages to the Greeks and Hebrews. He brushed away the "barbarians" in true cavalier fashion— "For their best music," he wrote in the preface, "is said to be hideous and astonishing sounds [*sic!*]. Of what importance then can it be to enquire into a practice that has not its foundation in science or system, or to know what are the sounds that most delight an Hottentot, a wild American, or even a more refined Chinese?"

This is, no doubt, a challenging statement. The "refined Chinese" had very definitely a system based on science, and all the ancient world from Egypt to the Pacific coast founded its music on science or system. This, of course, Sir John could hardly have known. But since he studied Hellenic sources, he should have known that the *chroai* or "shades" of Grecian scales with their manifold, often irrational steps were thoroughly Oriental and hence as "hideous" and inferior as all the music excluded from his gigantic work. He sneered at Oriental music, not because it was hideous, but because it was said to be hideous. He did not even know it and felt no urge to test the report. For the chapters on Greek and Hebrew music there were no witnesses and consequently no reports. The two sections were easily filled with learned quotations from literary sources well known to all the author's erudite contemporaries; the music itself hardly needed discussion; being biblical or Greek, it was to every reader perfect almost by definition.

Historians have ever since followed one of these two leads. Four years after Burney and Hawkins, Jean-Benjamin de La Borde's *Essai sur la Musique* of 1780 discusses again, as Martini's *Storia* had done, the Hebrews, "Chaldeans and other Oriental peoples," the Egyptians, and the Greeks. But there are also Chinese and Siamese, Arabs, Persians, and Turks, Negroes and many others. This Frenchman was truly a universalist. In comparison, Johann Nicolaus Forkel's *Allgemeine Geschichte der Musik* of 1788 was limited in scope: his early civilizations were Egyptian, Hebrew, Greek, and Roman.

Even the nineteenth century was split. F.-J. Fétis, in his *Histoire générale de la Musique* (1869) said expressly—and we should inscribe it on the lintels of our houses—"*L'histoire de la musique embrasse celle du genre humain*"—the history of music is the history of mankind. Accordingly, there are in Fétis sections, not only on India, China, and Japan, but also on Kalmucks, Kirghizes, and Kamchadals—just to give a small selection of his subjects. Yet John P. Hullah, who wrote a *History of Modern Music* in 1871, thought that, "much as the Orientals have or have had" a "music of their own," this music "as at present practised . . . has no charm, nor indeed meaning, for us." "The European system, though the exigencies of practice prevent its being absolutely true, is nearer the truth than any other." No charm, no meaning, more remote from the truth—these are indeed unmistakable answers to the egocentric question, "What does that music mean to me? Can I enjoy it?"

To be frank, even those who thought that the Orient and the primitives were a necessary part of music history knew very little of them. And the little they knew, from hearing, hearsay, or occasional samples, was not co-ordinated or connected with European traditions and concepts. In K. C. F. Krause's *Darstellungen aus der Geschichte der Musik* (1827), we read: "In antiquity, [which was] the childhood of music, only simple unadorned melody was known, as is the case today with such people as the Hindus, Chinese, Persians, and Arabs, who have not yet progressed beyond the childhood stage." This is truly Hegelian; it suggests Positivism and progress; and it also shows the conceit of the upstart, to say nothing of the profound ignorance disclosed in the notion that the Hindus, Persians, and Chinese sing only "simple, unadorned melody"—when they are in fact unrivaled masters of the art of highly adorned singing; it is they who leave simplicity to the lower forms of folk and children's song.

Even greater historians than Krause lost their sense of balance and their judgment. The reader who consults the first volume of the monumental *Geschichte der Musik* by August Wilhelm Ambros (1861) will find a whole *Buch* on the music of the *Culturvölker des Orients* and even of the primitives. But in these pages he also finds assertions such as: "Assyrian music seems never to have risen above the level of a mere sensual stimulus"; or the music of Babylon "was quite certainly [!] voluptuous, noisy, and far from simple beauty and noble form." As for Phoenician music, its main role was "to drown the cries of the victims who burned in the glowing arms of Moloch." How brutish! Even the hope that they might have mended their ways before old Ambros was reprinted in 1887 proved futile: the third, *"gänzlich umgearbeitete"* edition has left these lines intact. Supposing the editor knew nothing of the excavations in the Fertile Crescent between the Two Rivers, should he not have known from the Bible that King Hiram helped his friend King Solomon build the Temple in Jerusalem with skilled artists? And did not this very Temple introduce an impressive number of musical instruments from Phoenicia with, among them, soft-sounding harps and zithers?

The general failure of the universal music histories is all the more surprising in that an interest in non-Western music had unmistakably shown itself even before the times of Burney and Hawkins. Travel diaries in the eighteenth century had begun to supply a few specimens of native song, doubtful sources, perhaps, since they were noted down by untrained persons, who squeezed whatever they heard into the familiar scales and rhythms of Europe, just as their pencils sketched the natives themselves according to the Greek-inspired classical canons of proportions and movements. It was an epoch-making moment when Jean-Jacques Rousseau reprinted a few exotic melodies in his *Dictionnaire de Musique* (1768)—from Finland, from *les sauvages du Canada,* and from China. The last of these, as I have already mentioned, is the one that Weber, less than forty years later, copied for his *Turandot.*

In the decade after Rousseau Oriental musicology as a scholarly discipline was born when Father Joseph Amiot, a missionary in China, published in 1779 his *Mémoire sur la Musique des Chinois, tant anciens que modernes,* a book of the greatest value, which we still consult with profit and respect. Less than twenty years later, Napoleon invaded Egypt and caused the large number of French scholars in various fields whom he had brought with him to study the country in all its aspects. After years of additional research in the *Bibliothèque Nationale*, the results were united in a gigantic *Description de l'Egypte*, almost three of the twenty-five volumes being given up to music: (1) *Mémoire sur la Musique de l'antique Egypte*, (2) *De l'Etat actuel de l'Art musical en Egypte*, and (3) *Description historique, technique et littéraire, des Instrumens de Musique des Orientaux*. The author of these musical volumes was Guillaume-André Villoteau.

One cannot easily exaggerate the merits of these three volumes. They show careful observation, are thoroughly correct, and are free from the preconceived ideas of a European. Villoteau, it is true, had his prejudices when he set foot on Egypt's soil. But, after studying with a native music teacher, he came to recognize that correctness of intonation was not a monopoly of Western man (who in the course of a long evolution had changed the size of his musical intervals and wound up with an incontestably incorrect "equal temperament"). The European system was by no means—in Hullah's words—"nearer the truth than any other." Oriental music, Villoteau learned to understand, was basically different from ours but not inferior; it had its own scientific foundation and had therefore to be judged according to its own rules.

In the time between Amiot and Villoteau, the French pioneers in a new realm, an English High Court judge in Calcutta, William Jones, had begun to study the music of India. In 1784, he wrote *On the Musical Modes of the Hindoos*, of which a German translation by F. H. v. Dalberg came out in 1802 under the more general title *Ueber die Musik der Indier*. Dalberg added to the original text and appended a number of musical examples beyond the one melody that Jones had given. But when he quotes his chief collector, an English musician in India, as saying that he had had no small trouble in setting the tunes in a regular tempo, we cannot accept them without distrust and reservation.

This essay not being bibliographical, we need not follow up the subsequent attempts of the nineteenth century to understand and expound Oriental music. Suffice it to say that exotic musicology in its earlier stage covered almost all great Oriental civilizations, and that a good many of the studies published in those decades proved to be excellent works, classics in their kind.

Whether excellent or not, they all contributed to the same result: all the theoretical points gathered from native writings—the elusive pitches of China and Japan, the melodic and rhythmical patterns of India or the Muhammedan lands, the musical philosophies and cosmological systems of the East in general, were presented to Western readers as proofs that Oriental music was a serious and scientifically (or at least prescientifically) established matter. The musical instruments, too, were described and depicted in countless contributions. But the music, the subject proper, was conspicuously absent.

The reasons for this absence are evident. They can be found above all in the way Oriental music takes shape. Orientals do not compose with paper and pen. They create their pieces while dreamily humming and strumming; and even after polishing rugged passages they do not pencil a definitive version. When they play in public, they are not bound to an "authentic," printed form, to an *Urtext*. There is none. Producing and reproducing fuse into a delightful unity in which the well-wrought, mentally definite form and the momentary impulse reach a perfect balance. Any notation would spoil this equilibrium in the irrelevant interests of finality; it would destroy the potentialities of a free-flowing melody in favor of inert impersonality. True, there are a few native notations, in India as well as in the Far East and the Muhammedan world. But they are vague and inadequate, and are meant to assist recollection rather than study or performance. Be they frozen descriptive gestures, as *neumes,* or alphabet symbols, they render at best a meaningless skeleton where we Westerners want a striking likeness.

If no native notation strives for faithful recording, the Western script is limited in its own way. Our system of white or blackened ovals on or between the lines of a staff is rational although not entirely logical and (as many incurable reformers have pointed out) is insufficient even for Western needs. It is wholly insufficient for Eastern music. Anyone will easily see why this is so. The English alphabet may give satisfaction to English-reading people (or so we like to suppose); but when it comes to rendering Arabic letters we are at a loss to represent the three different H's, three S's, three T's of that language, for we have only three symbols to represent nine sounds. Nor can we Romanize a Sanskrit text without an array of tildes, dashes, and dots above or below the English letter to prevent our making the text unintelligible. Reading Oriental music from Western staff lines is quite as misleading as reading Oriental poetry in a twenty-six letter alphabet. The microtones in an octave (twenty-two in India against our twelve), the subtle shades of intonation, the countless mannerisms and fleeting ornaments which give life to Oriental melody, cannot be rendered. Simplification becomes falsification.

Worse: whoever uses an alphabet or a notation such as ours is lured often against his will into a fatal error. Forced to render the three Arabic T's by only one, he shuts his ear and mind to their differences, both in sound and in etymological importance, and treats them as equivalent. We have a good example closer at hand than Arabic and Sanskrit. Every day, we see French words in our papers; the rough spelling might be fairly correct, but the three accents of the originals are usually missing, and the accented words appear very often as similar unaccented words with a totally different meaning (as *l'an passé*, "last year," which becomes *l'an passe*, "the year goes by"; or Gabriel *Fauré*, who is no relative of Félix *Faure*). We miswrite, misread, and misunderstand.

The musical situation is analogous. Whoever compromises between an Oriental performance and the habitual thought of black and white ovals, on a five-line staff with a time signature, unsettles a good many Eastern pitches and beats and, often naively, resettles them on one or between two of our staff lines. Or again, ignoring the freedom of a melody, he forces a note on one of the three or four beats per measure that he takes for granted. We should not forget how much of musical perception is a matter of suggestion. And this suggestion is stronger, and more dangerous, where no efficient control, no methodical education, no discipline, is at hand to create the detached atmosphere of correct observation.

The established historians of European music should have provided this education and this atmosphere. But, alas, they did not seek to expand their horizons beyond Europe, and their playground was the library with its manuscripts and printed scores. The Orient was out of bounds; and so was any music composed to be heard rather than to be read. Why should any serious scholar engrossed in canons and organa stoop down to the crude, infantile singsong of savages? Alas, they did not know that canons are sung by palaeolithic Pygmies in Asia and Africa; nor that ancient Greeks and medieval men looked up admiringly to the Orient. Oriental and primitive musicology was neither encouraged nor assisted by the historians of music. Help came from other quarters.

It came in the eighteen-eighties.

The first of the founding fathers was an Englishman, Alexander J. Ellis. Far from being a musician, he was a prolific, versatile scholar, whose attention was focused mainly on phonetics and the reform of spelling. In the course of his research, he made himself familiar with acoustics and the psychology of hearing, and one day chanced to confront the thrilling problems of exotic scales with their unusual, awkward steps. It was fortunate that he had no musical ear and thus eluded the snobbish reliance on a sense so far from reliability as hearing. Instead, he used the objective methods of scientists and an ingenious computing system of *Cents* or hundredths of an equal-tempered semitone. The details of the system will hardly interest the readers of this essay. Its gist was the logarithmic transformation of the frequency numbers of individual tones into very simple distance figures independent of the clumsy, ungraphic, and ever-changing frequency ratios in exclusive use up to his time. The subjective perception of the Western musician was hereby eliminated: scientific observation replaced arbitrary, falsifying approximation.

The epoch-making publication of this method took place in Ellis' "Tonometrical Observations on some Existing Non-Harmonic Scales," a paper first printed in the *Proceedings of the Royal Society* (1884) and reprinted in the following year in the *Journal of the Society of Arts* under the simplified title "On the Musical Scales of Various Nations." In his own words, "The final conclusion is that the Musical Scale is not one, not 'natural,' nor even founded necessarily on the laws of the constitution of musical sound so beautifully worked out by Helmholtz, but very diverse, very artificial, and very capricious."

These studies were among the early contributions to a field of learning that was based on precise observation and measurement and was aimed at a scholarly independence of preconceived occidental standards.

The second founding father was Thomas A. Edison. By the time he was thirty years old he had begun to transform the vibrations of human voices into curves engraved in the wax coating of rotating cylinders. At first the sounds were blurred, harsh, and creaking. But the revolutionary invention had been made. Sound, with its characteristic inflections and even individual timbres, was recorded, reproduced, and preserved; the aural counterpart of photography had become reality.

The paths of Edison's phonograph and of the lore of exotic music converged in the eighties, when an eminent anthropologist and later Chief of the U. S. Bureau of Ethnology, Dr. Jesse Walter Fewkes, made use of such a machine in his studies of the settlements of southwestern Amerindians. A number of songs collected in the pueblos of the Zuñi in New Mexico were thus recorded, transcribed at home by the Harvard music-psychologist Benjamin Ives Gilman, and printed in Western notation in the first volume of the *Journal of American Archaeology and Ethnology* (1890). Two years later the German psychologist, Carl Stumpf, re-edited Gilman's work for the *Vierteljahrsschrift für Musikwissenschaft,* Vol. VIII. The new branch of learning was thus established both in this country and in Europe.

It must be said that Gilman's transcription bypassed Ellis' subtleties which had been expressly devised for the scale-conscious music of the great Oriental civilizations, but not for the inconsistent intonations of primitive melodies. All that Gilman did to show deviations from the Western system was to add plus or minus signs where a note was sensibly higher or lower. And Stumpf agreed with a quotation from Helmholtz: "Who would cut firewood with a razor?"

Half a generation after the founders, archives were established in a number of cities on either side of the Atlantic. (Their chronology is not quite certain since some count the age of an organized institute from the time it has a curator, an assistant, a technician, and a budget, while others compute from the year when the earliest recording finds its way into some museum, only to be lost, mildewed, and forgotten.) These archives were meant for the collection and conservation of exotic cylinders (and later discs) and for the encouragement of the use of recording machines on scientific expeditions. The author himself witnessed for decades how, with the Berlin *Phonogrammarchiv* as their headquarters, old Stumpf and his disciple Erich von Hornbostel persuaded departing explorers to add an Edison to the camera, to record the songs they might hear, and to bring them back for preservative treatment, dubbing, storage, transcription, and analysis. Dozens of weighty ethnological works of the early twentieth century include special chapters on music, unselfishly contributed by von Hornbostel. Along with him, and in the two decades since his death, devoted scholars all over the world have collected records, built phonographic archives, and published a literature of thousands of books and papers.

The new branch of learning—what was its name to be?

The Germans called it *Vergleichende Musikwissenschaft,* in analogy to *Vergleichende Sprachwissenschaft;* the Americans and English followed with *Comparative Musicology* and the French with *Musicologie comparée.*

These titles are of dubious significance. Every branch of knowledge must at bottom be comparative, for all our descriptions state similarities and differences, in the humanities no less than in the sciences; and in music history too, we cannot discuss Palestrina's masses without comparing them with Lasso's or Victoria's. Indeed, all our thinking is a form of comparison: to speak of a blue sky is to compare it with a gray one.

The name "Comparative Musicology" was perhaps acceptable fifty or sixty years ago when haphazard and incoherent bits of information were trickling in: a few Edison cylinders from North American Indians, a doubtfully notated melody from Mongolia, a performance given at some fair by a group of Siamese players. There were many differences and a few similarities in intervals, rhythms, moods, and singing styles. The earliest scholars in the field were faced with approximations and disparities—with a few bewildering, motley samples of an enormous stock as yet unknown. Unable to draw connecting lines at so early a date, they could not but compare their scanty findings: this is "like . . . ," and this is "unlike . . ."

After the discredit of Comparative Musicology as an acceptable title, some leading men in the field have begun to speak of Ethnomusicology or, in Germany, of *Musikalische Völkerkunde.* The English title is somewhat unwieldy and hard to explain to people who have no clear idea of musicol-

ogy even without a prefix. The *Musikalische Völkerkunde*
of the Germans seems to put an exaggerated stress on the
ethnological part of the aggregate. For an aggregate it is, not
only in name. The man who works in this field sits on the
fence between musicology and ethnology. This we must not
hold against him. One need only thumb through a cata-
logue of some modern university to find quite similar aggre-
gates: astrophysics, psychophysiology, paleobotany, and dozens of similar fusions. Rather than sit on intellectual fences,
we prefer to tear them down. The world, which we want to
explore, and man, whom we strive to understand, are too
complex to justify the departmental separation from which
our colleges suffer. The history of even Western music comes
to life only when the musicologist is aware of the unbreak-
able ties between music and man and his culture.

The name is at bottom irrelevant as long as it duly keeps
in evidence the part that relates to music. For the area of
study in question deals with music primarily, though it par-
takes of ethnology, too, and contributes to the understanding of primitive man. Actually, this ethnomusicology is not
confined to the primitive. It also embraces the middle and
high civilizations, like those of the Far East, India, and the
Muslim countries, which are not in the domain of ethnology.
This remark, I hope, will not encourage word-coiners to
speak of "Orientomusicology."

There is indeed no unified name comprehending all the
heterogeneous people who cross our path in this field: (1)
the high civilizations of the East, (2) the low and middle
civilizations, (3) and the remainders of low and middle civilizations in rustic parts of our own civilization. These three
groups have little in common except the negative quality of
differing from that which is just as vaguely and incorrectly
described as the West. Thus, the musical situation does not
differ from that in other similar disciplines. But the men devoted to Negro art or Chinese literature do not bother with
newfangled composites or -ologies; they soberly describe

themselves as historians of Negro art or of Chinese literature.

The only, though fateful, difference is that these historians are specialists trained in Sinology and Negro lore or else in the histories of art and of literature. In the musical field, circumstances have been less favorable. Of the founding fathers, one was a phonetician, one was an ethnologist, and two were psychologists. In the following generation, Erich von Hornbostel, the leading figure, was a chemist converted to psychology. And so forth. Only in the third generation do we find a few historians of music—of the West. Nothing could be more elucidating than to look over the twelve installments of an impressive *Bibliography of Asiatic Musics* by a group working under the guidance of William Lichtenwanger, published in *Notes* between 1947 and 1951; only a handful of the listed authors have a music-historical background.

This means that the whole enormous edifice of collecting, transcribing, teaching, and editing exotic music (or, in this case, Asiatic music), far from growing out of music history, has been erected outside, with little encouragement from the owners and tenants of the older building and often against their open resistance. The reason is twofold. The old humanistic background of Western education still provides a yardstick taken from the Greeks, or, better, from what older scholars fancied the Greeks to have been with Winkelmann's "serene simplicity and noble grandeur" still haunting studies and classrooms. This dogged aloofness of the illuminati excluded not only the primitives, but also people of the Eastern high civilizations as barbarians and—I quote correctly—as savages. Obsolete as these concepts and terms may be, they are depressingly persistent.

The second reason is the attitude, prevailing in quite a number of universities and colleges, of accepting the history of music—if it cannot be helped—but only as a negligible appendix to a school of music for the preparation, not of scholars, but of composers, conductors, players, and singers of modern Western music. Such a conservatory is indeed not the place for teaching the lore of Oriental or primitive music.

As matters stand, the persons attracted towards research in non-Western music must very often take refuge in Anthropology or Psychology departments, whose generous hospitality must be gratefully acknowledged and recommended for imitation to those departments of music that belong to a school of the humanities. Music different from ours is human too; and man is not confined to the West.

Scholarly interest in exotic music is not a desideratum, but a fact. It has grown beyond expectation, and it will stay. True, its academic permits of residence are not yet very numerous. But for all its hardships, it has in the seventy years of its life immensely widened our horizon—both musically and in many other ways—and no shortsighted opposition can rebuild around us the wall that it has broken down.

Thus the new branch needs no apology or letter of introduction. Once the word "savage," which no modern anthropologist uses any more, has disappeared from the language of our divisions of the humanities and departments of music, every student of musicology will be allowed an insight into the musical world outside our realm; and he will be given an opportunity, within the music departments, to do research and, eventually, to teach in this field.

Then, we shall no longer be in need of a new, unwieldy designation. The thing itself will be well enough known to be recognized under some simple, unpretentious name.

Musicology and Related Disciplines

By CARROLL C. PRATT

MUSICOLOGY AND RELATED DISCIPLINES

1. *Specialization in modern scholarship*

Comments and complaints about the high degree of specialization which has entered into all modern studies—into the humanities as well as the sciences—have become of late so widespread and numerous that they may obscure another trend which is in a quite different, if not opposite, direction. Just in proportion as a scholar feels obliged for whatever reason to narrow the scope of his inquiry, he becomes dependent on others for help in supplying some meaningful context for his work. French political satire written in quatrains during the seventeenth and eighteenth centuries, or the reflex action of the rear legs of *Rana palustris* (the pickerel frog) are topics which can hardly be exhausted in a lifetime of study, but they are also topics which have little significance unless they are viewed within the larger frameworks of French poetry and political history and of general physiology. Yet an authority in either of those topics might not dare utter a word outside of his own specialty, for any such word, if it is to be authoritative, can only be spoken by some other specialist. Many scholars today find themselves at times in full sympathetic agreement with the historian who said that the last twenty minutes of the Renaissance would be too vast a subject for any one man to know adequately.

Specialization of this kind is in many fields of study practically inevitable, for the amount of knowledge which lies on either side of a narrow path of inquiry is so immense that no one mind can possibly cope with it. The days when men like Leonardo and Goethe could deal effectively with many different kinds of subjects are probably gone forever, Spengler and Sorokin and Toynbee and their like to the contrary notwithstanding.

One of the trends designed to delay intense specialization

51

from going completely to seed has been the formation of groups of experts, each of whom from his particular angle works towards the center of some area. Medical groups replace the old family doctor who was supposed to diagnose and cure all the ills of both body and mind. Research contracts in the natural and social sciences are today rarely granted to a single individual. Groups of specialists are appointed to a task which no one member is expected to understand. In collaboration they pool resources in order to arrive at solutions which could hardly be reached by one person working alone.

The Renaissance, or any large area of study, no matter how briefly circumscribed in time or scope, needs for adequate comprehension all sorts of historians, students of religion and trade, artists and musicians, as well as scientists and philosophers of every kind and description. The advantages of this sort of collaboration, in an effort to offset the dangers of sterility inherent in overspecialization, are obvious enough. There are also grave disadvantages which may shortly become painfully apparent in American education and research. At the moment, however, it is important only to note the trend. It will be for the future to decide how to restore some balance between the pursuit of minute facts and the comprehension of general ideas.

Hardly any subject in the American university of today exemplifies better than musicology the necessity as well as the dangers of intense specialization. If the main task of musicology may be regarded as the analysis of musical style, it becomes obvious at once that every special discipline in the humanities, the social sciences, and the natural sciences, including mathematics, will have to be drawn upon at one time or another for a proper understanding of the tenacious and almost universal hold which music has had upon the human mind and heart.

The vast variety of musical expression must in some way reflect the well nigh infinite diversity and complexity of the human spirit. For him who loves music, that fact is obvious and delightful; and therefore for him there is no problem

nor bewilderment connected with his enjoyment. If you ask
him *why* he should want to listen to music, instead of rever-
ing you as a philosopher, he will probably laugh at you for a
fool, to paraphrase a similar illustration in James' chapter
on Instinct in the second volume of the *Principles* (p. 386 f).

> It takes, in short (says James), what Berkeley calls a mind
> debauched by learning to carry the process of making the
> natural seem strange, so far as to ask for the *why* of any in-
> stinctive act. To the metaphysician alone can such ques-
> tions occur as: Why do we smile, when pleased, and not
> scowl? Why are we unable to talk to a crowd as we talk to
> a single friend? Why does a particular maiden turn our
> wits so upside-down? The common man can only say, "*Of
> course* we smile, *of course* our heart palpitates at the sight
> of the crowd, *of course* we love the maiden, that beautiful
> soul clad in that perfect form, so palpably and flagrantly
> made from all eternity to be loved!"

But for the philosopher—in this case, the musicologist—the
fact of musical enjoyment is the occasion for trying to find
out the *why* of such pleasure. If the questions raised by the
musicologist seem to obscure the plain fact of enjoyment, so
likewise do all questions in philosophy tend to obscure and
confuse the everyday facts of life, which is no reason for doing away with philosophy, the love of knowledge, nor with
musicology, the knowledge of music.

The questions raised by musicology require for an answer, if indeed there can ever be an answer, the combined
efforts of a host of experts. It is impossible for any one person to combine within himself all of the qualifications
needed for the complete analysis and explanation of musical
style. What, then, does a person who calls himself a musicologist regard as his primary concern? What, in other words,
is a musicologist? An appeal to the dictionary does not fur-
nish an answer, for the word has not yet made the grade
either in Webster or Oxford. The German word *Musikwissenschaft* is perhaps the best indication of what has come to
be the English equivalent of that word. Yet no definition in
a dictionary would be adequate, for musicology, like all
modern scholarly pursuits, is best defined in relation to what

those people do who call themselves musicologists rather than to some conventional specification of an area of study.

What is a physicist? The dictionary calls him one who is versed in natural science. No physicist today, however, would dare say that he is versed in natural science. He may be a student of cosmic rays, an expert in field theory and relativity, a specialist in wind velocities and shock waves, etc. But outside of those narrow areas he would prefer to be regarded, with respect to natural science, as little more than an amateur.

What is a psychologist? The American Psychological Association is composed of many divisions. If a member in the division of physiological psychology, an expert let us say in the field of visual perception, were asked some question about the relation of learning theory to neurosis, he would probably shrug his shoulders with the remark that such a question should be turned over to a clinical psychologist. The latter, in turn, would want to pass on to someone else any question about extinction of conditioned reflexes,—and so on through the many divisions and subdivisions of modern psychology. It means little to say that psychology is the study of the mind, for it can be argued that the mind, oddly enough, is whatever psychologists occupy themselves with in their studies; and that occupation would surely not find itself properly defined in any dictionary.

Psychology and musicology are indeed somewhat alike in the way in which they sprawl all over the place. If musicology is defined in terms of what musicologists do, it would not be enough to inquire into the activities of any one scholar in the field, for different members of the profession are engaged in many different kinds of investigation.

2. The Central Task of Musicology

A major concentration of interests and activities on the part of American musicologists may be discovered by a quick perusal of the articles in the *Journal of the American Musi-*

cological Society from 1948 through 1953. Fifty-five of the sixty-seven major contributions, more than 80 per cent, fall into the category of historical studies, some of them delving into regions of remote and perhaps even dubious importance. This convergence of effort into one region has in certain quarters brought upon musicology the reproach of dealing too much with dry-as-dust antiquarianism, a charge that might be sustained were it not for the fact that (1) large numbers of studies of very different sorts in other journals belong properly in the area of musicology, and (2) analysis of musical style has to be made on music which has already made a place for itself, or might conceivably achieve a place if rediscovered. The treatment of the material must therefore inevitably be historical in its emphasis. It is consequently fair to say that the core of musicological research is history. A penetrating analysis of musical style, however, needs a formidable array of propaedeutic and auxiliary disciplines. The purpose of the following sections is to give some indication of the scope and significance of those disciplines insofar as they bear upon musicological research. The study of musicology, especially by American undergraduates, as one of the liberal and liberating arts is another matter which will be touched upon briefly at the end of this essay. At the moment the concern is primarily with the graduate student and young scholar who is preparing himself for a professional career in musicology.

3. *History*

It is obvious that historical studies should be from early till late the business as well as the pleasure of scholars in the field of musicology. There can be no end to the pursuit of information and ideas and interpretations about all places and times in the world which have any bearing on the understanding of every phase of music. It may be taken for granted, of course, that the scholar is thoroughly versed in the history of music, not as given in literary digests, but as taught in the atmosphere of the most severe standards of graduate study. The training and outlook thus gained in the classroom will be carried over by the student to his own more or less independent conquest of whatever historical knowledge relates to his special interests in music. This knowledge cannot be gained in the classroom, for departments of music have more than enough to do in their own domain; and in our compartmentalized system of instruction all related departments, such as those of history and of literature, generally find it impossible to offer courses designed for specialists in other disciplines. The student of musicology must therefore strive early in his career to reach the ideal of all graduate study, namely, self-instruction. The much-vaunted and sought-after commodity of integration is probably in any case much better achieved by the learner himself than by cross-departmental instruction.

The situation is analogous to the problem in medical training. The specialist in surgery or psychiatry is obliged to learn the tricks of his trade *after* his period of formal instruction is finished. Formal instruction can only hope to lay the basis in concepts, information and attitudes which will enable the student to stand upright and alone at the frontiers of knowledge.

4. Sociology

The kinds of history that are important to the musicologist are for the most part different from the more conventional accounts, no matter how detailed and accurate these latter may be. The student of musicology may indeed have to write his own history, after he has searched the sources for initial data, as has been done so impressively, for instance, in the case of Kirkpatrick's *Scarlatti* or Newman's *Wagner,* to cite the first examples that come to mind. What the musicologist needs is a sociology of the past, an account of social structures and hierarchies, the practices of patronage and support of the arts, an examination of religious attitudes and prejudices, educational systems, the hopes and ambitions of young people of all classes, etc.,—in short, as minute a record as possible of the cultural life of the period under investigation. If music and the makers of music are to some extent the product of their social environment, a thorough knowledge of that environment assumes a place of first-rate importance not only in understanding the lives of musicians, but also in striving for deeper insight into the styles of their compositions.

5. Biography

Biographies of great men serve many purposes beyond the pleasure they give to lovers of high gossip. Even such gossip, trivial and irrelevant as it may seem from some points of view, has its place in the early stages of a student's curiosity about science and art, for the telling of it in such books as J. W. N. Sullivan's *Beethoven* and *Newton* or De Tolnay's *Michelangelo* may lead the inquisitive reader straight into the concert hall or laboratory or the Sistine Chapel. There is every good reason to suppose that the consuming passion which some scholars develop for art or science had its origin in the interest aroused by the reading of the lives of great men. Who can read about the barren and solitary existence of Immanuel Kant without wanting to find out what went on in the mind of that strange recluse who rarely during his eighty years set foot outside his native town of Königsberg and whose daily afternoon walks, rain or shine, were so punctual that neighbors checked their timepieces as he passed their houses?

For musicological research, careful and critical study of biography has a very special and cogent purpose. Musical style can be studied from two quite different angles, both of which are essential for a scholarly and sympathetic appreciation of what makes music what it is and enables it to do what it does. The first approach has always been the chief method of musicological research and will undoubtedly remain so for a long time to come. It consists primarily in a minute examination of auditory and musical structure regarded as an independent entity with its own laws, properties, dependencies, internal coherence and consistencies, balance, proportions, lines and rhythms, et cetera almost ad infinitum. Yet this task, however difficult and time-consuming it may be, is only half, or some fraction or other, of the total account required for a proper appreciation of musical style. If as Bukofzer says, analysis may be thought of as composition in reverse, then the later stages of analysis move out of musicology proper into the domains of philosophy and psychology. An independent musical structure is a fiction, albeit necessary and legitimate enough for purposes of scientific study, but nevertheless lacking some of its most vital elements when treated apart from its source. Every musical idea began life in the mind of a composer, and a complete analysis, operating as it were in reverse, must therefore end up in the domain of biography.

It is often asserted, and presumably very widely believed, that music reveals more directly the inner life of the artist than does any other form of art. The aphorism that music is the language of emotion, however murky the meaning may become when examined critically, presents a challenge both to philosophy and to musicology in its clear implication that although emotion may have other avenues of communication, the medium of sound is the best. How the emotions and the inner life of the composer can be translated directly into the tonal patterns of music is a psychomusicological problem of the first order of magnitude. It will be referred to again briefly in the section on psychology. For the moment the point to be made is that from the point of view of musical analysis certain kinds of biographical data assume an importance far beyond that of idle and irrelevant gossip.

The same problem exists in the study of all forms of human creativity, although perhaps nowhere so plainly as in music. In the case of science, and particularly mathematics, it is frequently assumed that the relation between the man and what he does in the library and laboratory is negligible. Ideally science is completely impersonal. It deals only with brute facts, so that the conclusions based on such facts reveal therefore not the mind of the thinker, but rather the nature of the material with which he operates. In science we are brought face to face with physical reality, whereas in art we find ourselves in the realm of the human spirit. This view of science, still widely held by many scientists themselves, is of course partly true, otherwise the predictions and applications of technology would have no validity whatever. But it is not the whole truth. There is a respectable metaphysics which argues plausibly that the vast array of scientific discovery represents a magnificent flight of human imagination, but whether the flight has made contact with ultimate reality no one knows. There can be no kind of knowledge which is completely divorced from the characteristics of the knower.

Even in mathematics the human element plays an appreciable role, as Bertrand Russell and others have often been fond of pointing out. The history of the calculus, for example, cannot be separated from the intensely personal attitudes and discoveries of Leibniz and Newton, and the disputes between those two irascible giants still enter into the calculations of today.

The phrase "Newtonian physics" represents more than a way of honoring the accomplishments of a towering genius. It refers also to a unique cast and power of mind which made it possible for Newton, when he turned his attention to the observations which some of his contemporaries had been making on the behavior of terrestial and celestial bodies, to formulate laws of motion and gravitation. If today physicists and astronomers vacillate between Einsteinian and Newtonian conceptions of the universe, it is well to bear in mind that neither conception is based exclusively on sheer factual material. There is actually no such thing as a pure fact. A fact is always a function of its method, and a method is always a human contrivance. No theory in science, according to Conant, is ever overthrown or replaced by the discovery of new facts, but only by the creation of a better theory. The personal equation, some element of biography, must enter even into the most rigid of scientific disciplines. In the less exact sciences, such as the art of medicine, the human element assumes a correspondingly larger role.

Philosophy may be regarded as standing perhaps about halfway between art and science. The wise philosopher lays the foundation of his system in such a way that it will not be inconsistent with the science of his day. But above the foundation he raises a structure for which science has little or no material to offer. How does he proceed? Is the major part of his system built by guess and by chance? The usual answer to that question, especially when given by philosophers, has been no. The good philosopher is an expert in exact and mathematical logic, so that each step in his thinking is inexorably determined by the preceding one. The whole system is therefore an impersonal structure in the sense that the facts of science and the laws of logic serve to reveal the true nature of all things as they were created by the mind of God, not as they happen to have been conceived in the brain of a philosopher.

It is obvious today that this view, however noble it may be, states considerably less than the truth about the nature of scientific and philosophical thinking. The facts of science and the principles of logic have never been and probably never will be completely coercive over the mind of any thinker. The mind of man is endowed with desires and passions which upon occasion will express themselves in spite of almost any conceivable barrier that can be placed in their way. Facts and logic are powerful obstacles in the way of wishful thinking, but they can always be overcome when confronted by real strength of mind and purpose. The wish may be father to the thought even when the father is nowhere to be seen. Indeed it is the view of a good many authorities, especially those who are a bit cynical in their attitude towards philosophers, that it is the function of logic to conceal the wish which drives the thinker to his goal. Logic is a clever device skillfully designed to hide from the vulgar gaze the beliefs (= powerful emotions) which the philosopher already had before he began to construct his system. The philosopher therefore comes out by the very same door where he went in, but in making the circuit he deceives his readers, and probably himself, by his use of elegant logical defenses and his judicious selection of facts.

Yet before leaving this topic it should be said emphatically, in all fairness to scientists and philosophers both great and small, that the intent on their part to arrive at objective and impersonal truth warrants devout respect. To dismiss the results of their labors as mere wishful thinking is inexcusable levity and misrepresentation. The works of Schopenhauer and Berkeley and Descartes, and all the other great figures in the history of philosophy, deserve study and analysis in their own right without any consideration at all of the personal idiosyncrasies of their authors. Just as in the analysis of musical style, so in the study of philosophy, the systems under investigation are entitled to an exhaustive examination of their internal consistency and the logic of their formulation. Schopenhauer and Berkeley and Descartes have presented *Weltanschauungen* of tremendous sweep and scope. Their views have markedly influenced all subsequent thought, and this influence has been independent of the manner of men they happened to be. Yet for a full understanding of the underlying motives of their brainwork it is necessary to inquire into such matters as the childhood of Schopenhauer, the missionary work of Bishop Berkeley, and the solitary habits of Descartes in order to find out how those phases of their lives, together with their native intellectual capacities and emotional endowments, may have determined the complexion of their thought.

The items in this second phase of analysis are clearly biographical, not logical—the sort of biography, for example, which has made it possible to say that in all probability the pessimistic extremes to which Schopenhauer was frequently driven in his systematic treatises were in no small measure the result of his deeply melancholy temperament rather than of inescapable conclusions based on sound major and minor premises. The connection between his ideas and his psychophysiology is in many cases so close as to justify the assumption of some kind of cause and effect.

Any such connection between music and the temperament of the composer is more problematical and probably in any case harder to establish, because music, when not combined with words, is nonideational and nondiscursive. The task of the musicologist is therefore in this regard vastly more difficult, not only in the systematic analysis of musical structure, but more especially in the dangerous business of trying to relate the musical structure to the life and personality of the composer. No wonder the program-notes at concerts and the talks of radio commentators all too often seem like dreadful stuff to the scholars in the audience—and all the more reason for the training of more musicologists in the critical study of biography so that they will be able to blow away the chaff.

6. Languages

If the study of foreign languages is regarded as an important preparation for musicological research, it may clarify the aim of graduate training to indicate how this study will be useful. The knowledge of foreign languages can have several purposes, some of which may have little or no relevance to musicology.

The mere knowledge of languages presumably has per se considerable cultural and social value. It is certainly a desirable and enviable ability, both at home and abroad, to shift easily from one language to another. And have we not all been reminded in recent advertisements how quickly our social prestige will soar if over cocktails we can converse with the distinguished foreign ambassador in his own tongue or recall without the trace of accent some of the bright remarks we heard in Rome or Paris yesterday afternoon? The gift of tongues must be a constant source of a very pleasant and justifiable feeling of superiority. This particular value, however, is of no concern in the training of music scholars, partly for the reason that the whole matter should have been taken care of in the secondary schools. Dr. Penfield, the famous neurologist, has recently given evidence that for most people the capacity for learning to speak foreign languages begins to fall off in the early teens.

The myth that the study of languages, particularly Greek and Latin, trains the mind has long since been largely exploded. There is no one subject which, as a formal discipline, is unique in the capacity to train the mind. It is the act of study itself rather than the content of the study which serves to strengthen the brain. Transfer of training takes place only across disciplines which have elements in common. A knowledge of mathematics has enormous transfer to the study of science for the good and sufficient reason that in the latter constant application is made of the very same knowledge acquired in the former. In this sense there must be some transfer from one language to another, and perhaps in particular from Latin to English, although not nearly so much as from mathematics to the special sciences. How does the knowledge of the use of the ablative case in Latin help one to write better English? Churchill by his own confession is pretty much of a stumblebum in every language except his own, but that shortcoming is certainly nowhere evident in his speeches and writing.

The most frequent argument in defense of language requirements is based, of course, on the amount of research published in foreign journals with which graduate students should presumably be acquainted. During the middle and latter part of the nineteenth century, when graduate work was striving for a firmer footing in American colleges, the young scholar hoped to spend at least a year or two of study abroad, and was regarded in any case as well-nigh illiterate if he could not read French and German. Europe was the source of his scholarly and scientific materials as well as his inspiration. To some extent the same attitude still prevails and must be counted among the influences which continue to support the study of foreign languages at the graduate level. Yet even here the time spent in boning up a reading knowledge of French and German might in certain disciplines be more profitably devoted to other activities, particularly in the case of those victims of the requirement for whom languages are a mystery and a nuisance.

For at least two very good reasons scientists today are relying less and less on the study of original sources. (1) The amount of research published in every subdivision of science is now so voluminous that no one person can hope to keep pace with it even in one or two languages, let alone a dozen or more. Summaries are absolutely essential, and in some disciplines the task of abstracting and translating articles from all over the world is very thoroughly and efficiently done. (2) Most of the standard books in science, certainly all of the great classics, are translated into English. No American student of acoustics, for example, would ever think of reading Helmholtz's *Die Lehre von den Tonempfindungen* in the original, for Ellis' *Sensations of Tone* is an excellent translation, and is also full of valuable footnotes and appendices not found in the original.

The style of an original work is of no great importance for scientists, so long as in translation the meaning is clear enough. Many scientists actually frown on writing which seems to them "literary," for they feel that attractiveness of style may confer upon the meaning an increment of appeal which is undeserved. (The same attitude is occasionally found even among philosophers, as witness their attitude toward the beautiful prose of Santayana). The reputations of fine writers like Eddington in physics or William James in psychology are not infrequently regarded by men in those fields as enhanced far beyond the intrinsic importance of what they had to say. Rumor has it that some years ago a hard-bitten senior professor in the Division of Philosophy and Psychology at Harvard was chided by the dean of the faculty for his repeated refusals to recommend promotions for the younger men. "I'd venture the guess," said the dean, "that if you had been here in the days when young William James was up for promotion, you would not have given your approval." "You're damned right I wouldn't," came the quick retort.

In the humanities the use of translations and summaries as shortcuts to the meanings of original texts is an entirely different matter. When undertaken for the benefit of the public at large, translations obviously have their place; but if done by and for the company of scholars themselves, any unnecessary tampering with original documents would be regarded as a violation of the very essence of humanistic research. In all of the arts the manner of expressing an idea is part of the quality of the idea itself. Translation of the idea into another medium is at best a poor substitute; at worst, it can be tantamount to aesthetic debauchery. Style and idea are too closely interwoven to permit of separation. In the scholarly study of the humanities a mastery of as many languages as possible is therefore of the highest importance.

What is true of the humanities in general with respect to the study of documents in the original language applies with even greater force to musicology. At all times and in all lands music has more frequently than not been associated with words. One has only to cite folk songs, plainsong and chant, indeed almost all church music, French chansons, opera, and countless other examples that will come readily to mind. Only in recent centuries in Western civilization has pure music, absolute music, achieved a firm and independent status. To analyze musical structures without painstaking reference to the meaning and sounds of the words that go with them would plainly lead to an incomplete and often erroneous understanding of their stylistic properties.

These last paragraphs would seem at first glance to contradict the arguments of the first paragraphs of this section. Not quite. Graduate training in the United States may soon stand at the crossroads with respect to the place of language studies in the curriculum. The influence and prestige of the natural sciences and the narrow practicality of some of their spokesmen have already seriously undermined the humanities. In some cases the men in the humanities have themselves done their cause more harm than good by using the wrong arguments in support of their claims. It is a weak and deplorable defense of the classics to argue, for example, that a knowledge of Latin roots is helpful to biologists and pharmacists in memorizing the nomenclature of their materials.

To define the liberal arts on the basis of their utility is likely to call forth from cynical realists the question, What is your evidence? The kind of evidence asked for in such a question is not easy to formulate in any manner which will impress those who pose the query. I am myself profoundly convinced that the utilitarian value of the liberal arts is greater than that of any other human activity, but that faith is largely intuitive. It will take decades, perhaps centuries, of research by scholars in the humanities to "prove" that "where there is no vision, the people perish." In the meantime, the most, or for that matter, the best that the supporters of the liberal arts can do for their cause is to insist that the good, the true, and the beautiful are either good in themselves or—no good at all.

Words and music have always been closely interrelated. The musicologist must therefore be an expert in philology as well as in *Musikwissenschaft*. In the present fluid and uncertain state of graduate requirements in our American universities it would seem best for those who speak on behalf of departments of music to point out that a mastery of languages is fully as important for the musicologist as for the scholar in literature or any other field of the humanities. The inseparable fusion of verbal and tonal attributes constitutes the stuff out of which most music is made. Any other arguments in defense of language-studies in departments of music would be superfluous, if not downright dangerous.

7. *Literature and the Fine Arts*

The case for literature, as well as for all the fine arts, as a supplement to the professional studies of the musicologist is clear and uncomplicated. If "whatsoever things were written aforetime were written for our learning," surely the musicologist less than almost any other specialist in art history would want to be exempt from the obligation and pleasure of that kind of learning.

The atmosphere and influence of literature create the milieu in which music and every other form of art are born. The interrelations of the arts within their common matrix are important items in the study of style; but here too, as in most other fields of learning, the evils of overspecialization become apparent. Ideally the history of each art should be taught in relation to the development of every other art; but such an assignment is too formidable for one person to undertake. The young scholar in musicology will have to go ahead pretty much on his own. It would be a great achievement on the part of American musicology if, in contrast to the scholarly studies in most of the humanities, it could by a concerted effort maintain a kind of lateral vision so that the relation of music to the other arts should never be lost sight of.

Collaboration between students of music and of literature might conceivably be more profitable and productive than almost any other kind of joint enterprise in the domain of art criticism and analysis. "Writing is not literature," said Stopford Brooke in his *Primer of English Literature,* "unless it gives to the reader a pleasure which arises not only from the things said, but from the way in which they are said; and that pleasure is only given when the words are carefully or curiously or beautifully put together into sentences." One of the main tasks of literary analysis is the discovery of why it is that certain combinations of words are beautiful and give pleasure, whereas other combinations fail. The analogy to music is very close, but a direct concern with their mutual similarities, in spite of the intimate association between words and music down the centuries, has all too frequently fallen into no-scholar's-land. If a few musicologists and philologists could work together to cultivate that land, it would almost certainly yield a rich harvest.

Finally it is worth pointing out that an alert musicologist with a wide acquaintance with literature would be able to turn up all kinds of references to music, as Barzun has done in his *Pleasures of Music*. Writers and poets are people, too, and their ideas about music are neither better nor worse than those of the next layman; but their ability to find words for their ideas, especially when they happen to be ideas about an art which many people feel it is foolish or too difficult to talk about, should be seized upon by the musicologist as a valuable source of material. Common sense is sometimes right, perhaps more often wrong; but those predicates can not be established until common sense has been subjected to systematic study. Music may not be the food of love, nor love seeking for a word, nor a kind of counting performed by the mind, and its charms may not soothe a savage breast. Yet if these phrases, and scores of others like them, are received with pleasure and approval by the layman, the musicologist cannot afford to toss them aside as so much nonsense. It will be a long time before we know what music *does* to people, before we can describe the *function* of music as well as the form. In the meantime, the search for an answer might well include a critical examination of what articulate people have to say about music and the way it affects them.

8. Philosophy, Psychology, and Aesthetics

If the views of writers and poets about music have any significance for the serious student, it surely must follow that any such student should give far more time and thought to the detailed and systematic ideas on art and music which have been formulated by those philosophers and psychologists whose interests have included the study of aesthetics. The ability of philosophers and psychologists to give expression to their ideas does not in general equal in felicity the professional writers' command of words; but in spite of that, or perhaps because of it, their concepts are usually clear, even when the supporting arguments are difficult to follow.

Philosophers as well as writers are for the most part laymen, or at best, amateurs in the arts; but this disadvantage, if it really is one, is compensated for on the part of many philosophers by long and arduous study of the history and problems of aesthetics. A philosopher or psychologist may, as a matter of fact, like neither painting nor music, yet acquire the skill of learned discourse about both. A physician does not have to love disease in order to understand it. It can even be argued that anyone who has a passion for art and is deeply immersed in it disqualifies himself as critic and scholar. Disinterested scholarship implies some degree of emotional detachment from the object under investigation —not so much so as to bring about psychical overdistance, but certainly enough to hold in check the dangers of intense ego-involvement.

The amount of philosophical speculation which has taken art as its object is so great that the average student of musicology may well be baffled to know where and how to wade into it. Fortunately most departments of philosophy and some departments of psychology can offer him assistance in this problem, for their courses and even their more advanced training in aesthetics rarely insist upon specialized prerequisites; and although their instruction is designed primarily for students of philosophy, the musicologist will ordinarily not be handicapped, because what he may lack in philosophical background can be made up for by a strong desire and determination to understand what philosophers have had to say about art in general and music in particular.

Most great philosophers have written their aesthetics almost as an afterthought, or rather, as a belated effort to com-

plete and round out their systems of metaphysics and episte-
mology. It will therefore usually be necessary for the musicologist to become pretty well grounded in the general systematic views of the author in order to follow what often
seems like tortuous and far-fetched reasonings when the author begins to grapple with the problems of aesthetics.

Small details, of course, are for students of philosophy
rather than the musicologist to study and evaluate. The latter
can afford to forget, for example, the definition of a Pytha-
gorean comma, but he must certainly make himself familiar
with the number-schemes which the disciples of Pythagoras
used in an effort to explain, not the harmony of the spheres,
but the relation between mathematics and music. That relation has haunted the minds of philosophers and mathe-
maticians from that day to this. The recent attempt by the
late Harvard mathematician, George Birkhoff, to develop in
his *Aesthetic Measure* a formula for the relative merit of
works of art, including music, may be regarded as a brilliant
failure; but it will not be the last one in the long search for a
number-scheme which will reduce the relations among the
elements of an art object to quantitative specification.

The aesthetics of Plato is derived logically from his metaphysics, and for that reason has frequently been condemned
as a glaring example of elegant reasoning done without
sympathetic regard to the intrinsic value and beauty of art.
Yet the views of Plato with respect to the role of formalism
in art have had a tenacious hold upon the minds of artists,
critics, and philosophers for well over two thousand years.
The shoptalk of artists about balance, contrast, harmony,
proportion, weight, line, contour, rhythm, et cetera ad infinitum, sound, as a matter of fact, like a popularized version
of some of the chapters in *The Republic*. The logic of Plato,
or rather his premises, may have been wrong, as he himself
suspected; but his conclusions have an appeal which cannot
easily be resisted.

The works of Hegel on aesthetics present a lively challenge
to every aspect of *Kunstwissenschaft*. His concept of idealiza-

tion in art has been called by several authorities the greatest single contribution ever made to the theory of art. Hegel, in contrast to most if not all of his predecessors, gave compelling evidence in support of a transcendent quality of art far beyond the intrinsic properties of the form of the object itself. His famous doctrine of art cycles—symbolic through classical to romantic—is buttressed by an impressive knowledge of history. But is it actually true that art runs in cycles or that the merit of an object of art derives from associative reinforcements of the form? In the last analysis the philosopher, in dealing with such questions, must appeal to the art scholar, for neither one alone commands enough of the intellectual tools required to forge the answers. In this respect the philosopher, in so far as Hegel deals with music, cannot turn to the musician or composer, but only to the musicologist who, in addition to his own specialized equipment, has saturated himself in Hegelian dialectics.

The same comments apply with even greater force to the aesthetics of Schopenhauer. Wagner said that he carried a copy of *Die Welt als Wille und Vorstellung* in his pocket for months at a time, and that no writer on art had ever impressed him so profoundly and filled him with such deep admiration. Whether Wagner's attachment to the writings of Schopenhauer had anything to do with the musical ideas in *Tristan* and *Meistersinger,* as Wagner said it did, is open to humorous doubt; but the lofty position ascribed to music by Schopenhauer, which Wagner naturally greatly approved, is again a matter for musicologists to take seriously.

Schopenhauer argued that the human will, which in the context of his philosophy means all forms of emotional striving, is a revelation of ultimate reality. Everything else is subjective perception, the eternal flux of shifting phenomena. Our little life is surrounded by shadows. How is it possible, then, to know reality? Kant and Berkeley had been driven to the conclusion that reality, in this sense, is beyond the range of human cognition. The melancholy Schopenhauer could not accept any such forlorn and fatalistic conclusion.

The key to the problem, he said, lies in an understanding of music, for music is in immediate contact with reality. It is a direct copy of the will, the *Ding an sich*. His arguments are romantic and even mystical, yet they have impressed many a tough-minded logician. If scholars have been led astray by the seductive fallacies of Schopenhauer, it behooves the musicologist to rid the scholars, particularly the logicians, of their rhapsodical errors.

These examples, chosen almost at random, serve merely as an illustration of the scope and kind of problems in aesthetics which have aroused the interest of many great philosophers. The wide influence which philosophy has always had in the history of human thought and culture justifies a more important place than of late it has enjoyed in the American scheme of instruction. It may be owing to the current neglect of philosophy that musicologists have been far more historical than philosophical in the way they have approached their special studies. Be that as it may, it would seem to go almost without saying that a philosophy of art and music uninformed by the expert knowledge of art scholars wants precision, just as a musicology innocent of philosophy lacks background and generality. Both need mutual reinforcement. Musicologists, in particular, if they are to fulfill their role as teachers of a great liberal art to a generation of students who have picked up on the run a formidable acquaintance with music of all kinds and descriptions, need in the classroom the wisdom of philosophy more than the facts of specialized research, however important these latter may be in their proper place.

The situation with respect to psychology in relation to musicology is somewhat different and at present possibly less important. Most philosophers keep fairly well abreast of developments in modern psychology, so that by concentrating more on philosophy the musicologist can presumably pick up enough psychology, even if at second hand. Philosophy and psychology generally approach their problems—in many cases the same ones—from different directions: philosophy, *von oben nach unten,* as Fechner put it; psychology, *von unten nach oben.* The latter procedure tries to pile up facts in the hope that out of them will emerge an irrefutable theory; the former starts with a theory from which it is hoped inescapable facts can be deduced. It is obvious today that both procedures are necessary, but since in the last analysis they undoubtedly represent an ultimate difference between the philosophical and the scientific temper of mind, they will probably always move along partly divided and to some extent irreconcilable paths down to the end of all learning.

The foundations of a scientific study of aesthetics—aesthetics in the laboratory—began with investigations which Fechner first reported in his monograph *Zur experimentalen Aesthetik* (1871), and then elaborated in greater detail in his *Vorschule der Aesthetik.* The father of psychophysics carried over into experimental aesthetics the same methods which most authorities, with the notable exception of James, have believed gave to psychology, by way of psychophysics, a secure basis for all future development along quantitative lines of research. In aesthetics these methods were applied by Fechner with tireless energy to minute analyses of the feeling-tone of the golden section and of all manner of simple geometric forms, of colors and tones in various combinations, etc. In spite of the accumulation of a mass of well-tested facts, no theory of any importance seemed to emerge. Most philosophers and some psychologists would be inclined to say about this sort of busy work in aesthetics what James said about psychophysics. For most of Fechner's prolific writings James had profound respect, but for the studies in psychophysics he had no stomach.

> The Fechnerian *Massformel* and the conception of it as an ultimate 'psychophysic law' will remain an 'idol of the den,' if ever there was one. Fechner himself indeed was a German *Gelehrter* of the ideal type, at once simple and shrewd, a mystic and an experimentalist, homely and daring, and as loyal to facts as to his theories. But it would be terrible if even such a dear old man as this could saddle our Science forever with his patient whimsies, and, in a

world so full of more nutritious objects of attention, compel all future students to plough through the difficulties, not only of his own works, but of the still drier ones written in his refutation. Those who desire this dreadful literature can find it; it has a 'disciplinary value;' but I will not even enumerate it in a footnote. The only amusing part of it is that Fechner's critics should always feel bound, after smiting his theories hip and thigh and leaving not a stick of them standing, to wind up by saying that nevertheless to him belongs the *imperishable glory*, of first formulating them and thereby turning psychology into an exact science,

> " 'And everybody praised the duke
> Who this great fight did win.'
> 'But what good came of it at last?'
> Quoth little Peterkin.
> 'Why, that I cannot tell,' said he,
> 'But 'twas a famous victory!' " [1]

There is one area of psychological inquiry, however, which is of central importance to aesthetics, especially since philosophy has nothing whatever to offer—except more words added to the thousands of words already spilled forth over the topic ever since it was first introduced by Aristotle. It is not possible to know just what Aristotle meant by *Katharsis*, beyond the obvious relation which it has to emotion in art. But to say that drama, or any other form of art, can purge the emotions does little more than state a problem. It certainly does not settle it. What does it mean to purge an emotion? Where is the emotion, in the object or in the person? Is it perhaps a relation between the two, or possibly only *Scheingefühl?* Or is there in art any emotion at all which physiologists or psychologists could identify by that term?

These questions are as hotly debated today as they ever were, and many psychologists often feel about them the way James did when, at the end of his famous chapter on emotion, he threw up his hands in despair over the experiences which he called the subtler emotions. If Chopin's highest praise of

[1] William James, *Principles*, I, 549.

a new piece of music, said James, was *"rien ne me choque,"* then aesthetic emotions would seem to have very little connection with the viscera, in contrast to the emotions of deep bodily reverberation which are so well taken care of by the James-Lange Theory. Yet the answer to these questions may not be far off, for physiology and psychology are now reporting a wealth of new material about emotion gained by methods which have only recently become available. Whatever the outcome, musicologists will be vitally concerned, if for no other reason than to know what to say about the assertion that music is the language of emotion.

Even if it were possible to dismiss that assertion as merely a pretty phrase, no student of art can ignore the belief, so widespread as to be almost universal, that works of art reveal in palpable form the inner life of man. The belief may be so self-evident as to deserve the high rank of platitude; but if so, the psychological mechanism by which the subjective is made objective, by which inner mood is transformed into outer reality, still remains obscure. The analysis of musical style, considered as an outer reality, leaves unanswered the question as to how the original idea of the composer can be permanently embodied in tonal structure. The answer may lie in the sort of psychobiography which Freud and his followers have developed.

The life of the soul or mind, the total personality of the individual, to use the current psychological terminology, is today regarded as made up of thought and action which at the surface are designed to conceal from public view, as well as from the individual himself, the true nature of underlying motives. Consciousness and behavior are both conceived of as rationalizations which have transformed the inner and lower impulses of man into socially acceptable practice. A man's personality is the part which he plays on life's stage, a mask, *persona,* in which the latent content of the mind is made manifest to outer view in the form of symbols which partially disguise the meaning of the latent content. The task of the psychiatrist and clinical psychologist, in the analysis and diagnosis of a patient, is to penetrate the outer shell of personality in order to find out what is going on in the hidden depths of the unconscious. The task of the scholar in his analysis of art forms is from this point of view very much the same.

All art is manifest content. Music is an elaborately developed projective technique, to use the jargon of clinical psychology, which if correctly interpreted reveals the latent content of the composer's mind. But how can the manifest content be interpreted? Music is nondiscursive. It has no meaning in the sense that words have meaning. Yet we have seen that philosophers and critics, lovers of music as well as musicians themselves, are as one in proclaiming tonal art the supreme manifestation of the soul of mankind. Are the Freudians wrong in their insistence on symbolism as the major key for unlocking the mysteries of mind? Symbolism is full of meaning, and its application to the analysis of human behavior has had an enormous influence on all modern thought. But a symbol without meaning is a contradiction in terms. Perhaps Schopenhauer was right. Music may not be a symbol at all but, rather, a direct copy of the will, the thing itself. These problems are too important for the musicologist to leave solely to philosophers and psychologists to deal with.

9. Physics, Physiology, and Psychology

The chief relation between musicology and the natural sciences lies in the domain of acoustics. If one accepts, for the purpose of the present discussion, Santayana's division of aesthetic experience into material, form, and expression, it is clear that form and expression are the major concern of all the humanities and some of the social sciences. The *material* of art, on the other hand—the sensory processes of vision and audition—is the point of departure for large areas of investigation in physics, physiology, and psychology. The adequate stimuli to light and sound are the wave frequencies and amplitudes of radiant energy and of air particles which impinge upon the eye and ear. These events, by conventional definition, are physical; and until recent years they constituted a major portion of instruction in all departments of physics. Before these physical events are transformed into light and sound, they must pass through the human nervous system.

The translation of physical events into neural excitation is plainly a problem for physiology. Physiologists and physicists, however, both rely upon psychologists—and to some extent upon artists—for a systematic description of the range and variety of colors and sounds for which physical and physiological correlates are required. If the human ear, for example, can distinguish some 300,000 pure tones, to say nothing of tones and noises produced by complex waveforms, the physiologist is faced with the difficult task of finding out how the physical correlates of those small differences are transmitted to the eighth (auditory) nerve by way of the mechanisms of the outer, middle, and inner ear in such a way as to preserve intact the qualitative and intensive attributes of those differences when they are delivered and perceived at the central region of projection. This problem, the central problem in all theories of hearing, has now been taken over almost exclusively by psychologists, or physiological psychologists, as they prefer to be called. Their great god is Helmholtz, who, although by *Fach* primarily a physicist, brought together in masterly fashion in his *Sensations of Tone* all the available evidence—much of it the product of his own research—in the three fields of physics, physiology, and psychology.

Science, like every other human activity, has its fads and fashions. Research in physics today naturally follows to a very considerable extent the pattern set by the writing and teaching done by men of established reputation. Young physicists are consequently devoting most of their energy to the study of atomic and nuclear particles, and the courses which in turn these young men like to offer to their students, both graduates and undergraduates, deal largely with preparation and training for research in the same direction. The familiar topics of yesterday—heat, light, sound, mechanics, electricity and magnetism, etc.—have all but disappeared from college catalogues. It would be difficult to find anywhere now a whole course devoted to acoustics, and probably not a single one planned for musicians, such as those which Saunders used to give at Harvard, or D. C. Miller at the Case School of Applied Science. The topic of sound, for most physicists today, is taken care of by a chapter in an elementary text and a lecture or two in the introductory course. The rest is silence.

The new generation of physiologists also hear and read very little about sound. Chapters and lectures on the ear find their place somewhere in the curriculum, but except for a few specialists the subject is soon put aside in favor of more detailed studies of nerve, cell, and glandular action, or for the far more practical research needed in the training of medical students, and supported by government grants. If a physiologist or medical student specializes in sensory mechanisms, he usually takes on the whole array of cutaneous and kinaesthetic senses in addition to the ear, eye, nose, and throat. It is obvious that such a person, especially if engaged in actual medical practice, must have a relatively limited knowledge of the ear compared with the research worker who devotes his whole life to acoustics.

As a result of one of the current fashions in psychology, there are now a number of men who actually are giving over practically all of their time to a study of every relevant aspect of hearing—the sound waves, the auditory mechanisms, and the perceived properties of tone and noise. In 1930, Wever and Bray, working in the Princeton psychological laboratory, hit upon the brilliant idea of amplifying, by means of specially constructed electronic devices, the action potentials set up by a tone or noise led into the eighth nerve of a cat. As the impulses came off the nerve they were electrically reproduced in a loudspeaker for any doubting Thomas to hear. There right before his ears were tones over a wide range of frequencies, and also sounds of the human voice reproduced with such fidelity that the listener could easily tell who was speaking into the cat's ear. These results, now known as the Wever-Bray effect, were novel and exciting. They answered a number of questions and made possible a critical re-examination of the views of Helmholtz, which for lack of any new evidence, had gone more or less unchallenged for more than sixty years; but as so often is the case, the results raised as many problems as they settled. A nerve, for example, can only conduct about one thousand impulses per second, because the refractory period of recovery precludes faster transmission; but on the cat-telephone-loudspeaker it was possible to hear tones of five thousand cycles per second, and the normal human ear can hear twenty thousand cycles.

The men who pursued these new directions of research, most of them psychologists, found it necessary to become masters in their own right of the whole field of acoustics, for the physicists and physiologists who might have helped them had wandered off in other directions. It has thus come about that the best research and courses in theories of hearing, which perforce now include nearly all of acoustics, are at present found in departments of psychology. Neff at Chicago, Licklider at Massachusetts Institute of Technology, Wever at Princeton, Stevens at Harvard—these are the men with whose contributions to acoustics it would be well for some musicologists, especially those whose interests include the material of music, to become familiar. Their writings tend for the most part to be highly technical, but adequate summaries can be found in most of the more advanced texts in experimental psychology, or better still, in a book like Geldard's *The Human Senses*.

In purely psychological, as contrasted with physical and physiological, studies of pitch, intensity, rhythm, scales, fusion, melody, cadence, intervals, consonance and dissonance, etc.—how old-fashioned these topics seem!—nothing particularly impressive has been reported in recent years. The groundwork in the phenomenology of tone was well laid by the older investigators, and it is to them that musicologists should still turn for instruction. Stumpf's two-volume *Tonpsychologie,* unfortunately never translated, is the standard work, although much of it is now out of date. R. M. Ogden's *Hearing* is a later and more useful source, as is also Haydon's *Introduction to Musicology.* But on no account should the serious student of musicology fail to have near at hand a copy of Ellis' translation of Helmholtz' great masterpiece. He might do no more than skim the chapters on physics and physiology, for those subjects are now brought much more up-to-date in newer texts; but he should read carefully the sections on the phenomenology of tone, if for no other reason than to enjoy the excursions which Helmholtz found himself unable to resist into such matters as Greek scales, Oriental music, the history of temperament and tuning, the use and misuse of instruments in combination, organs and organ pipes, pianos and piano makers, etc.

10. *Anthropology, Archaeology, and Ethnology*

A huge but rather amorphous field of scientific and historical inquiry of vital concern to certain phases of musicology is variously represented in special divisions and subdivisions of those disciplines which deal with comparative studies of man, races, languages, cultures, religions, moral codes, etc. If we may be allowed to doubt that in the beginning "the whole earth was of one language, and of one speech," we can still note that music has been spared the more extreme cleavages heard in Babel. The language of music is said to be universal—possibly because, since it has nothing to say, everyone can understand it; yet the tonal surface of non-Western music, and also a good deal of contemporary Western music, frequently sounds strange, and perhaps for that reason, generally strident and irritating. The unexpected and baffling way in which the notes are put together interferes with anticipated communication and understanding of musical intent. Analysis of new directions in contemporary music and of the history and status of non-Western music presents a problem whose surface has hardly been scratched.

In this area, until recently almost completely neglected as compared with the amount of effort devoted to the study of older musical culture in Western civilization, the musicologist will again have to practice the ideal of all advanced scholarship, namely, self-education. The problems as well as the boundaries of archaeology and all related disciplines are ill-defined. All that one can say with any degree of certainty is that the extent of ground to be covered is staggering to contemplate. The specialists themselves are compelled to limit sharply the scope of their inquiries, and in the great majority of cases are conditioned by their professional training in such a way as to pursue lines of investigation which rarely have anything to do with music. Their subjects, moreover, are not represented at all in many American universities, so that even if the musicologist wanted to take a course or two in ethnology and anthropology, it would be only by rare good chance that he would find himself and those courses in the same institution.

The young scholar whose interests in music extend into out-of-the-way regions of the world will have to learn to beg, borrow, and steal his materials, most of which may turn out to be of little help to him. In desperation he will have to become his own anthropologist, just as psychologists interested in acoustics had to become their own physicists, although in their case for quite different reasons. In good time a few capable and earnest scholars will then be able to lay firm foundations for a genuine science of comparative musicology.

11. *Choice of Related Disciplines*

The foregoing sections will serve to indicate some of the more important ramifications of musicology into related areas of knowledge. The list is by no means exhaustive, but is certainly long enough to confirm the statement made earlier, namely, that hardly any subject in the American university of today exemplifies better than musicology the necessity as well as the dangers of intense specialization. Specialization on the part of the individual scholar is in point of fact not only necessary; if he wants to make original contributions to knowledge, it is unavoidable, for he cannot possibly be adequate to the wide range of highly developed disciplines required to give to analysis of musical style the generality which it must ultimately achieve. And therein, of course, lies the danger, a danger which is more apparent in the humanities, and especially musicology, than it is in the natural sciences. The latter have a powerful safety device for their protection.

Modern science has built for itself an imposing edifice, every stone of which is held in place by the cement of theoretical concepts which in respect to their validity can be tested by methods not available to the humanities. The method of testing scientific validity can be illustrated by the familiar concept of force. In the dictionary, "force" is defined in more than a dozen different ways; but in physics, $F = ma$. If a billiard ball at rest on a smooth surface is hit by a ball in motion, the former will start to move; and even casual observation reveals at once that the speed of movement is some function both of the speed and of the mass of the object that struck it. Refinement of such observations under carefully controlled conditions furnished the data upon which Newton formulated his second law of motion. The validity of the physical concept of force can thus be tested by retracing the steps taken in its formulation back to the initial observations. If the process of retracing fails at any point, then something is wrong with the definition. A scientific definition is *nothing but* the operations, both experimental and logical, which have been performed during the process of constructing theory out of fact. Anything else that creeps into the definition is technical nonsense.

This method of scientific validation, which Bridgman has

called *operationism*, protects the individual worker, no matter how highly specialized or far removed from immediate reality his research may be, from adding useless or meaningless ornaments to the solid structure of science. The young scholar, even in his highest flights of fancy, must always find his way back to earth, for the rules of the game he plays are strict in this regard. His head may be in the clouds, *but his feet must be on the ground.* The method is not infallible, as the history of science abundantly shows; but it has brought us closer to the truth of the world, whatever that elusive commodity may be, than any other device yet discovered.

As soon as the young scholar in musicology, on the other hand, pursues his own independent research, he runs the risk, in his effort to discover something new, of wandering so far afield that the way back to music, the point of departure, may be lost. Reproaches like the one sometimes made about metaphysics, that it resembles the attempt of a blind man to catch a black cat in a dark alley where no cat actually exists, have not yet been hurled at musicology, although the remark that "heard melodies are sweet, but those unheard are musicology," points in the same direction.

How can the dilemma be solved? There is of course no perfect solution, otherwise we should not hear on all sides so much talk about the dangers of overspecialization. In the study of musicology it goes without saying—or perhaps it does not go quite without saying—that first, last, and always the point of return as well as the point of departure must be music itself. Music is the thing.

Any attempt to bring about a separation of musicology from other musical activities in university, college, school, or conservatory should be prevented at all costs, for the results would only increase the evils of specialization, decrease the chances of mutual aid, and give musicology a false identity. The difference between musicologists, on the one hand, and composers and performers, on the other, is one more of degree than of kind. Musicologists play and sing and sometimes write a little music, perhaps just for fun; and most composers today and some performers have certainly read a book or two, perhaps quite carefully. The extraordinary rise in standards of taste and performance in American colleges over the last thirty years or so has been brought about by men who were not, strictly speaking, musicologists; but they were members of college faculties and were possessed of a good deal of solid learning as well as enthusiasm for a cause. Let not such men be cut off from constant association with those whose primary concern is *Musikwissenschaft*, lest the latter lose contact with the everyday realities of music.

Musicology as an organized discipline in American universities is still small and young enough to exercise some control and guidance over its own destiny in a manner far more effective than similar efforts would be in the much larger and more cumbersome learned societies. Members of the American Musicological Society who have any responsibility for research and instruction in graduate departments could profitably band together, in some informal way, for the purpose of plotting those procedures which would assist the young scholar in selecting the more nutritious and rewarding areas of investigation.

The chief protection against overspecialization in musicology, paradoxically enough, lies in the desirability, if not the necessity, of linking musical research with adjacent fields of specialization. Familiarity with two or three lines of inquiry should tend to reduce the likelihood of running into cul-de-sacs. Courses and books and men in those subjects which have some bearing on musicology would almost certainly be closer to music proper than would the research of the specialist who confines himself exclusively to his own narrow topic. Every graduate student would therefore be well advised to choose a minor subject in a related discipline in addition to his major requirements. It is here that the senior professors, on the basis of their own wisdom and past experience and in frequent consultation with colleagues in other institutions, could offer invaluable aid. The best minor subject for a student at Columbia might be quite different from the best one offered at California, but knowledge of this sort is difficult for the student to get at without assistance from the senior men who make it their business to assemble such information and impart their findings both to their own students and to their colleagues in the American Musicological Society.

It is patently obvious from all that has been said in the preceding sections that the choice of major and minor subjects to be pursued by the graduate student will have to be severely restricted in accordance with his capacities and his dominant interests. The student who has acquired a good background in various branches of the humanities during his undergraduate years should make capital of what he has learned when he takes up his professional studies in musicology, whereas the student who has taken a good deal of physics or philosophy or psychology should not allow those subjects to fade away. Such remarks are platitudinous, but in view of the formidable choice of related disciplines which confronts the professional scholar in music, they need to be kept constantly in mind by himself and his senior advisers.

12. Undergraduate Instruction

From the foregoing it is obvious, the author hopes, that the professional musicologist must be a man of broad learning and deep sympathy. These attributes in close relationship can rarely be attained outside of the rigorous discipline of a large university where departmental interchange and communication could be common phenomena. The musicologist-in-training, moreover, in order to meet the challenge imposed by the field's rigid requirements, will seldom be a young student. He will pursue his studies on the graduate level of university instruction or, though exceptionally, on an equal level of independent study. Maturity, scholarship and balanced judgment—the musicologist's stock in trade—are seldom acquired in the early years of college life.

It has been necessary, therefore, to base this essay upon

the resources and facilities of graduate training, to relate it
to the kind of preparation ideally needed by the young
scholar planning to become a professional musicologist. Presumably the number of students who will ever embark upon
such a career will be small. Yet musicology should always be
aware of younger persons who may be attracted to it, who
may feel (at a tender academic or physical age) its power of
elucidating musical and artistic phenomena, who will re-
joice at the opportunity of using combined fields of knowledge.

Musical scholarship cannot ignore anyone who sincerely
wishes to invade the "science" of musical art. Consequently
the esotericism that is frequently associated with musicology
should be dissipated, and musicologists of eminence and understanding should be humble in the knowledge they possess. This means, in turn, that younger students, sensitive to
the appeal of musicology, should be exposed to its values
and encouraged to embrace it if they are equal to its demands. And by extension this proposition poses to the professors an obvious yet seldom realized responsibility—to hu-
manize (not popularize) their subject with imagination and
insight. The usual musical subjects taught on the undergraduate level are not musicology, but they contribute to it
and become part of it. The intelligent sympathy of the professors, as they confront younger students in their formative
years, is therefore indispensable if the discipline is to be
wisely represented.

Every generation of college students loves sooner or later
to take it out on professors of literature who go so deeply
into historical and literary analysis that they seem to forget,
from the point of view of the students, what it is they are
analyzing. The students want to learn more about literature
per se, but instead they get a whole semester of minute analysis of every conceivable factor which has any possible relation to every shade of meaning of every word and phrase in
one poem. The job done on them is a scholarly one, but they
will have none of it, or only a small portion.

Psychology over the last decades has been faced with a

similar problem. Students in undergraduate courses learned a great deal about nerve action, visual acuities and auditory thresholds, conditioned and unconditioned reflexes, and then complained that they were told nothing about the varieties of human nature, its motives, passions, capacities, conflicts, etc. Their professors were either indifferent to the complaints, or stumped by them. Many had been trained in Germany, where it was accepted gospel that mind or human nature as a total *Gestalt* could not be fathomed until the elements of mind—sensations and their attributes along with their physiological correlates—were thoroughly analyzed. The students wanted Freud and they were given Fechner. In recent years a drastic revision has taken place in almost all texts and introductory courses. The best ones have not in any way lowered their standards, but have been brought rather more in line with the legitimate curiosity of modern students about human nature. The topics of sensation and reflex are postponed until the senior year, or even until graduate study. The students in the earlier courses, most of whom of course have no intention whatever of going on with the subject, hear more about Freud, and are no worse off for hearing much less about Fechner.

The physical sciences are better off in this respect. Most of their students, except those in the elementary and survey courses, plan to make professional use of their knowledge in engineering, scientific research, or medicine. Their work is designed not so much to develop well-rounded gentlemen as to produce experts in science and technology.[2] The courses in science have a further advantage. They follow a step-wise progression such that work at one level presupposes a mastery of preceding levels. The humanities are not blessed or cursed with such a hierarchy,—and are therefore not in a position to dictate to their students.

When Plato spoke of the supreme importance of music in

[2] The writer's experience in this connection is worthy of mention. He has found among scientists more of the genuine amateur's love of music and the arts than among his friends who profess the humanities. What is the reason?

the education of youth, it is reasonable to suppose that he did not have musicology in mind.

> The good body [said Plato] cannot by any bodily excellence improve the soul, but the good soul can by her excellence improve the body; and for the good soul the highest virtue is love of music. Musical training is a more potent instrument than any other, because rhythm and harmony find their way into the inner places of the soul, on which they mightily fasten, imparting grace, and making the soul of him who is rightly educated graceful, or of him who is ill-educated ungraceful. And those whom we have to educate can never become musical until we and they know the essential forms of temperance, courage, and liberality, and can recognize them and their images wherever they are found.[3]

A large measure of Platonic philosophy should constantly inform the decisions of those professors of music who have the responsibility of planning undergraduate instruction.

Performers, composers, and scholars all have their place in every department of music. Scholars, composers, and performers have their place in every school and conservatory of music. Any member of a music faculty in an American college who in this day and age ignores scholarship deserves to be replaced at once; and any musicologist who in an undergraduate course fails to increase his students' love of music is equally lacking in the exercise of his fundamental responsibility.

[3] Plato, *The Republic*, Book III.